Life Long Memories

Vikram Batchu

Vikram Batchu
1st Edition

Publication Date: July 2026
Price: 499 /-
ISBN: 978-93-7164-571-3
Published by:
Adhyyan Books
Office No. 589,
Opposite Vivanta by Taj,
DDA SFS. Pocket-1, Dwarka,
Sec-22, New Delhi-110077
Website: http://adhyyanbooks.com
E-mail: contact@adhyyanbooks.com

Printed at: Repro Printers, Delhi

"It is better to perform one's own dharma imperfectly than to perform another's perfectly."

— *Bhagavad Gita, 3.35*

"Men have become the tools of their tools."

— *Henry David Thoreau, Walden, 1854*

Author's Note

There is a particular kind of silence that falls when something you have spent years building becomes, in an instant, unremarkable.

I encountered mine on an ordinary Wednesday evening in a conference room in Dubai. A colleague had asked a system a question, a question about regulatory exposure across multiple jurisdictions in the financial sector — and the system had answered it. Not with perfect accuracy. But with sufficient accuracy. With the kind of structured, cross-referenced, precisely qualified response that would have taken a senior analyst the better part of a week to assemble.

The room moved on. Quickly. The way rooms always move on. I did not.

I have spent more than twenty years at the intersection of technology, data, and institutional transformation. I have helped banks redesign the architecture of trust. I have helped governments build systems capable of perceiving what individual human analysts cannot perceive. I have sat in rooms where the future was being shaped by people who did not yet know they were shaping it. I thought I understood the pace of change. I believed I was prepared for it.

But in that conference room I felt something I had not anticipated. Not anxiety. Not professional threat. Something quieter and more unsettling: the visceral sense that the ground itself had shifted beneath everyone in the room, and that I was, inexplicably, the only one who had noticed the movement.

This book is my attempt to understand that feeling, to trace what it reveals about the civilisation we are building and the responsibilities we are accumulating without quite admitting it.

Not as a technical treatise, there are better-equipped people for that work. Not as a prediction, I have spent enough time in technology to know how swiftly predictions become embarrassments. But as a reckoning with what it means to inhabit a world that has begun to remember differently. Because that is what I believe is actually happening. Not artificial intelligence in the science-fiction sense. Not automation anxiety, not capitalism's latest drama with labour. Something more subtle and more consequential: we have built systems that hold the accumulated reasoning of human civilisation, its science, its medicine, its law, its literature, its millennia of ethical argument, and made that accumulated reasoning available, on demand, to anyone with a question. We have externalised not just data but the capacity to synthesise it. We have externalised not just information but the very faculty of inference.

The Bhagavad Gita poses a question that has stayed with me throughout the writing of this book. When Arjuna stands at Kurukshetra, unable to raise his bow, paralysed by the magnitude of what he is about to do, Krishna does not counsel retreat. He counsels understanding: act according to your dharma, not from personal calculation or fear, but from a clear and unflinching apprehension of what you owe to this particular moment.

I am not Arjuna. But the question felt apposite. What is owed to this moment? By those of us who build these systems, who advise the institutions that deploy them, who sit in those conference rooms as the future is being quietly decided? What is the dharma of the technologist in the age of the machine?

This book is an attempt to answer that honestly. I write it as a practitioner — two decades of building things that actually had to work in the world. I write it as a strategist, having watched organisations discover, often too late, that the forces they dismissed were precisely the ones that mattered most. And I write it, most deeply, as a father.

Suhana asked me once why the phone needed to know things. She was seven. She wanted to understand what was inside it. I explained, inadequately, I think, about servers and algorithms and vast stores of text. She listened with the patient courtesy of a child who already senses the adult is not quite answering the question. Then she rephrased it: does it remember?

I have been thinking about that ever since. If these pages help you think about it too, not to resolve it, which may not be possible, but to hold it with the gravity it deserves then they will have done what I intended.

The argument, stated plainly: these systems are not artificial intelligence in the science-fiction sense. They are the externalization of human memory, centuries of accumulated human reasoning, made synthesizable on demand. What follows is about what kind of humans and institutions we become around that. The name at the front of this book is not the initialism. It is the meaning underneath it: Life Long Memories.

Vikram Batchu

Dubai, 2026

Gratitude & Acknowledgements

This book exists because life allowed it to exist.

Before ideas, before words, before memory itself, there was grace.

I offer my deepest gratitude to the **Universe**, the **Creator**, and to **God**, in whatever form truth reveals itself, for the gift of awareness, curiosity, and the capacity to reflect. For the lives we are given, and for the questions those lives compel us to ask.

To my **parents** and **in-laws**, who shaped my values long before I had the language to name them, who built the foundations on which every thought in these pages rests. Thank you for the quiet inheritance of integrity, patience, and love. Everything I understand about the importance of roots, I learned from you.

To my **family**, for being my constant in a world that never stops changing. Your presence is the thing I am most grateful for, and the thing I would miss most if it were absent.

To my beloved partner and wife, **Preethi**, your strength, patience, and belief are my grounding. Your presence brought balance to thought and calm to uncertainty. You read every draft with unflinching honesty, asked the questions that pushed the thinking deeper, and quietly held everything together while this book found its shape. This work carries your fingerprints on every page. There are no adequate words for that debt, so I offer instead what I hope is its equivalent: everything else.

To our extraordinary daughter, **Suhana**, you are the future this book quietly contemplates. May you grow not only intelligent, but wise. Not only capable, but aligned. Not only successful, but purposeful. You asked me once why the phone needed to know things. I wrote this book trying to answer you. I am still not entirely sure I have, but I am grateful, beyond measure, for the question.

To the friends who listened, questioned, challenged, and stood beside me across the years of this work, this book carries your echoes. You know who you are. I hope you know what it meant.

To my colleagues across two decades of work in technology, data, and enterprise transformation, the clients who gave me problems worth solving, the collaborators who taught me what I did not yet know, the critics who demanded more precision, and the occasional sceptic who was simply right. Much of what I understand about what happens when systems meet people came from watching you navigate that encounter with everything you had.

To the researchers, historians, journalists, and philosophers whose work has shaped every chapter of these pages, your scholarship is the scaffolding on which this argument rests. I have tried to represent your work with fidelity and care. Any errors are entirely mine.

And finally, my gratitude to **Life itself** — for reminding me, again and again, that intelligence without humility is hollow, and that progress without Dharma is incomplete.

The work continues. So does the gratitude.

About the Author

Vikram Batchu is a technology strategist and enterprise transformation leader with more than twenty years of experience working at the intersection of data, artificial intelligence, and organisational change. He has led large-scale digital and data programmes across some of the world's most complex institutions including banks, government ministries, and healthcare systems — across Asia, the Middle East, and Europe.

His career has given him an unusually direct view of what happens when powerful technology meets real institutional constraints: the moments when transformation succeeds, the more frequent moments when it fails, and the rarer moments when it reveals something unexpected about the nature of the problem being solved. It is from these specific, grounded encounters — not from theory — that his thinking about artificial intelligence and its human consequences has developed.

He has advised C-suite executives and government ministers on technology strategy, led teams across cultures and disciplines, and worked in environments where the gap between what technology is technically capable of and what organisations are humanly ready for is sometimes vast. It is this gap, and the human wisdom required to navigate it, that gave rise to this book.

He writes and speaks on the intersection of technology, ethics, and organisational leadership. He believes that the most important conversations about artificial intelligence are not primarily technical — they are about values, governance, and the kind of world we are choosing to build.

He lives in the United Arab Emirates with his wife Preethi and their daughter Suhana, who continues to ask questions for which he is still finding the answers, and whom he expects will find better ones.

A note on the people in this book: the professionals who appear in the narrative vignettes, Raj, Maya, Ananya, Arjun, Aarav, Rahul, *and* Sara, *are composite figures drawn from direct professional experience over two decades.*

Each represents a pattern I have encountered many times across sectors and organisations, not a single individual. Their names are invented. Their situations are not.

Contents

Preface

Why This Book Exists

"Things are in the saddle, and ride mankind."

— *Ralph Waldo Emerson, Ode Inscribed to W. H. Channing, 1847*

In the third century before the common era, the ancient city of Alexandria was home to the greatest library the world had ever produced. At its height, the Library of Alexandria held somewhere between forty thousand and seven hundred thousand scrolls — historians still argue about the number — containing the accumulated written knowledge of the Greek, Egyptian, Persian, and other ancient worlds. Scholars came from across the Mediterranean to study there. Euclid formulated his geometry in Alexandria. Eratosthenes calculated the circumference of the earth there with astonishing accuracy. Archimedes may have studied there. The library was not merely a repository. It was an engine of civilisation — the place where knowledge from different cultures was brought into conversation, synthesised, and extended.

Then it burned. Not in a single dramatic conflagration — history is rarely so neat — but in a series of destructions over several centuries, each one removing more of what had been gathered there. Julius Caesar may have accidentally ignited part of it during his campaign in 48 BC. The Roman emperor

Aurelian is thought to have damaged it in the third century. The library's final decline came gradually, through neglect, through the conversion of Alexandria to Christianity, through the dispersal of its scholars, until what had been the memory of the ancient world was simply gone.

What was lost is unknowable, which is part of what makes the loss so haunting. We know from fragments and references in surviving texts that works existed which we will never read. Scientific treatises, philosophical dialogues, mathematical proofs, literary epics, historical accounts; ideas that might have accelerated human understanding by centuries, extinguished before they could propagate. The astronomer Aristarchus of Samos argued that the earth revolved around the sun nearly two thousand years before Copernicus. His full arguments did not survive. We know he made them only because others mentioned them. The thought was had. The paper burned.

***

I think about Alexandria often. Not in the way that scholars think about it, tracing its specific historical significance, but in the way that a person thinks about a story that has lodged itself in the imagination and keeps returning at unexpected moments. I think about it because I believe we are living through a moment that is, in some fundamental ways, its mirror image — a moment not of catastrophic memory loss but of something stranger and more unsettling: the sudden, unexpected, and perhaps permanent extension of memory itself.

The first time I felt this unsettlement was not during a conference presentation on the future of artificial intelligence, though I have sat through many of those. It was during an ordinary late working evening, my desk covered with papers I had been reading for a client engagement, a question forming in my mind that I had been circling for several days. I typed the question into one of the new systems, almost as an experiment, not expecting much. What I got back was not merely an answer. It was a synthesis: the question I had been circling, approached from four different disciplines simultaneously, with the key tensions identified and the most promising lines of inquiry highlighted. It was, as best as I could judge, correct. And it had taken the system perhaps twelve seconds.

What unsettled me was not the speed. I had become accustomed to technology making things faster. What unsettled me was something subtler: the recognition that the synthesis I had just received would have taken me, working carefully, perhaps two days. Not because I lacked the intelligence. Because I would have had to move through a sequence of disciplines one at a time, reading papers, following citations, building up the picture incrementally. The system had done something different. It had held the entire picture at once — not because it was smarter in any meaningful sense, but because it had access to a form of memory that mine simply did not.

There is an ancient word for the question this raises. In Sanskrit, it is dharma — a word so rich and layered that it resists translation into any single English equivalent. It means, at various levels, duty, right conduct, the order that sustains the cosmos. Its root is dhr — to hold, to sustain. What the concept asks, across every context in which it appears, is this: given who you are and what the situation requires, what does it mean to act rightly? Not what is convenient, not what is rewarding, not what seems inevitable — but what your role and your nature and this particular moment require of you.

I write this not only as a technologist and strategist who has spent two decades helping organisations navigate transformations they did not fully anticipate. I write it as a father. Preethi — my wife, my first reader, my most honest critic — and I have a daughter named Suhana. She was seven when she asked, on a Wednesday evening, why the phone needed to know so many things. She was not anxious about it. She was curious. But the question she asked was more precise than most adults have managed, because she had not yet learned to assume that the answers to uncomfortable questions belong to someone else.

Suhana will inherit extraordinary capability. She may grow up in a world where answers arrive instantly, where information scarcity has been replaced by something more complicated. And the question that this possibility raises — which is the question this book is about — is not what that capability will do to her. It is what she, and we, will choose to do with it. The tools are not the story. The choices we make with the tools are the story.

I want to be clear about what this book is not. It is not a prediction. I have spent enough time watching confident predictions about technology fail in specific and instructive ways to be cautious about making my own. Predictions require a stability in the underlying trajectory that the technology we are discussing has not yet demonstrated. It continues to change faster than our ability to fully characterise it.

This is also not a book about artificial intelligence in the technical sense. I am not primarily interested in transformers, or parameters, or gradient descent. I am interested in what happens to human life — to the texture of professional work, to the nature of education, to the structure of power, to the practice of democracy, to the meaning of expertise — when memory becomes external, and synthesis becomes instant. These are not technical questions. They are human ones, and they have antecedents in every previous moment when a technology reorganised the relationship between what humans know and how they act.

Writing this book has been its own form of navigating the transition. I have used these tools throughout — not to write the prose, which remains mine, but to research, to surface historical material I would have spent weeks finding otherwise, to check my reasoning against perspectives I would have missed. I have tried to use them the way I believe all of us will eventually need to learn to use them: as memory extended, not judgment replaced. The synthesis in these pages, and the errors, are my own.

What follows is organised around four movements: Shock, Fracture, Reckoning, and Choice. They are not stages in a tidy progression. They are simultaneous registers of an experience that is happening to all of us at once — even if we are at different stages of noticing it. You may find yourself in different chapters at different moments. That is as it should be.

One more thing, before we begin. The professionals in these pages — Raj, Maya, Ananya, Arjun — all have networks, credentials, and proximity to opportunity that most of the people most affected by this transition do not have. This book is written from inside that privilege, about a transformation whose costs fall unevenly outside it. That is worth saying at the beginning, not the end.

Let us begin.

PROLOGUE

Life Long Memories

"The eye altering, alters all."

— *William Blake, The Mental Traveller, c. 1803*

Consider the name. Large Language Model. It is the phrase the world has settled on to describe one of the most consequential technologies in human history. Engineers chose it because it is accurate: these systems are large (trained on enormous datasets), they model language (they predict and generate text), and they use statistical patterns derived from that language to do something that looks, under certain conditions, remarkably like thinking.

I want to propose a different name. Not as a marketing exercise, not as a philosophical provocation, but as a genuine attempt to see the thing more clearly. Because how we name a thing shapes how we relate to it. The name Large Language Model makes these systems sound like very sophisticated autocomplete. What they are, in practice, is something that has no clear precedent in the history of human tools.

For thousands of years, human beings fought a losing battle against forgetting. We were extraordinary at producing knowledge, at observing the natural world, at reasoning about mathematics and philosophy and ethics and art, but we were poor at retaining it. Individual human memory is unreliable, selective, and mortal. A lifetime of hard-won understanding dies with the person who accumulated it, leaving behind only what survived the twin vicissitudes of time and chance unless it was written down. Unless someone preserved it. Unless it survived.

Every tool we developed for this purpose changed what we could collectively think. Writing allowed ideas to survive their thinkers. Libraries allowed ideas from different times and places to exist in proximity, enabling the connections between them. The telegraph and mass printing allowed ideas to propagate faster than any institution could mediate. The internet allowed the entire preserved record to be queried from anywhere on earth. Each development was not merely a storage improvement. Each one fundamentally changed what humanity could build on, because it changed what humanity could remember.

What these new systems add is something that, in retrospect, seems almost obvious — and yet represents a genuine discontinuity. Previous memory technologies stored the record and made it searchable. They did not synthesise it. The scholar who used a library still had to move through the record manually — reading, comparing, connecting — because synthesis was what the human mind brought to the material. The library was the memory. The scholar was the intelligence.

These new systems do both simultaneously. They hold the record — imperfectly, with lacunae and biases that reflect their training — and they perform a version of the synthesis that was previously exclusively human. Not perfectly. Not in the way a trained expert synthesises, with a lifetime of contextual knowledge and professional judgment.

But well enough, in enough domains, to change the nature of what individual humans need to do to participate in knowledge work.

The first time most people experienced this, they barely registered what was happening. A student asked a question and got an answer that would have taken a library visit to construct. A professional needed a summary and received one that saved three hours. A writer wanted background research and found it waiting for them, already organised, in less time than it would take to open a browser. The tool seemed like a convenience. A labour-saving device. A faster search.

The distinction matters enormously, and I want to dwell on it for a moment before we proceed, because the rest of this book depends on it. The difference between a better search engine and a system that synthesises human memory is not a difference of degree. It is a difference of kind. A better search engine helps you find where the knowledge is. A system that synthesises memory changes what it means for an individual human to know things in the first place.

Consider what happened in the history of reading when the printing press arrived. Before Gutenberg, a book was rare, expensive, and typically encountered in supervised contexts — a monastery, a university, a wealthy patron's library. The relationship between a reader and a text was mediated by scarcity. You did not idly pick up a book and read it the way you might pick up a conversation. You sought out specific texts with intention, in specific places, under specific conditions. Reading was itself a kind of ceremony.

The printing press did not just make books cheaper. It changed the nature of the reader's relationship to knowledge. Books became domestic objects. Private reading became possible. The reader was no longer dependent on an institution to mediate their access to text. They could encounter ideas directly, without supervision, and form their own judgments about them. This was, in the view of many historians, one of the preconditions for the Protestant Reformation, for the Scientific Revolution, for the Enlightenment because all of those movements depended on individuals being willing to form independent judgments in domains where authority had previously been absolute.

A tool that changes access to knowledge changes the nature of the knower.

We did not build artificial intelligence. We built civilisation's external memory.

These systems do not merely provide answers. They reveal us. They reflect back the accumulated weight of human thought — its genius and its cruelty, its wisdom and its prejudice, its highest aspirations and its most persistent failures. When you ask one of these systems a question about history or science or ethics or art, you are not merely querying a database. You are encountering a compressed version of what human civilisation has collectively said about that subject, weighted in ways that reflect whose voices were most present in the training data, whose perspectives were most documented, whose knowledge was most legible to the system that learned from it.

This is why the experience of interacting with these systems often feels numinous in a way that is hard to articulate. Not quite like using a tool. Not quite like talking to a person. Something liminal — hovering at the threshold between instrument and interlocutor — or something genuinely new, for which we do not yet have the right vocabulary. The strangeness is appropriate. What we are encountering is genuinely strange: a non-human system that carries within it the imprint of millions of human minds, none of them present, all of them somehow there.

This book is not about machines becoming human. It is not about the arrival of artificial consciousness, which I believe we are not close to and which I think is in any case a distraction from the questions that are already present. It is about something simpler and in some ways more urgent: the reorganisation of human civilisation that is already underway as a result of having built something that functions as its external memory.

***

THE QUESTION THAT DOESN'T GO AWAY

There is a question that returns to me whenever I spend time thinking carefully about what these systems represent. It is not a technical question. It is a civilisational one, and it has the quality of being simultaneously urgent and almost impossible to answer directly: are we building tools, or are we building infrastructure?

The distinction matters. Tools are optional. You pick them up when you need them and put them down when you don't. They extend human capability in specific, bounded ways, and the person using the tool retains full agency over whether to use it and how. A hammer is a tool. A calculator is a tool. Even the internet, in its early form, felt something like a tool, a resource you consulted and then closed.

Infrastructure is different. Infrastructure becomes the condition within which other things happen. You do not choose to "use" an electrical grid — you live and work in a world organised around the assumption that electricity is available, and the absence of that assumption would make your ordinary activities impossible. The grid is not a tool you pick up. It is the substrate on which your life runs.

Language models are beginning to behave like infrastructure rather than tools. They are being embedded in the systems that process healthcare decisions, that route financial transactions, that curate the information environments of billions of people, that assist in the drafting of legal documents and policy papers and educational content. They are becoming, quietly and rapidly, part of the substrate on which significant portions of human civilisation are beginning to run.

When a technology becomes infrastructure, the questions that govern it change. We do not regulate hammers. We do regulate electrical grids, water systems, financial systems — because when infrastructure fails or is captured or is operated in ways that serve narrow interests at the expense of broad ones, the consequences are not bounded. They cascade through the systems that depend on the infrastructure, affecting people who never chose to depend on it and who may not even be aware that they do.

The governance frameworks we have for AI systems are, almost universally, tool-governance frameworks: they regulate the technology as if it were optional, as if individuals could simply choose not to depend on it, as if its failures would be local and bounded and recoverable. These frameworks are already inadequate, and they are becoming more inadequate as the technology becomes more embedded.

I am not arguing for any specific regulatory approach here that would require a different book, one with more policy expertise than I possess. I am arguing for a clarity of recognition: that the infrastructure question is the right frame for thinking about what governance is actually needed. The choices made in the next few years about how AI infrastructure is owned, governed, and made accountable are choices of the kind that societies make only a few times per century, and that tend to shape the distribution of power, opportunity, and vulnerability for generations.

This is not a reason for despair. It is a reason for seriousness. The choices about electrical grid regulation, about financial system oversight, about public health infrastructure — these were also made in periods of great uncertainty, by people who did not fully understand what they were deciding, in the face of intense opposition from those who benefited from the absence of regulation. The choices were made imperfectly. They were revised over time. They produced systems that, for all their flaws, are considerably better than what unregulated infrastructure had delivered. The process is possible. It requires sustained engagement from people who care about outcomes that are shared rather than outcomes that benefit whoever happens to be best positioned.

That asking — that requirement — is what this book is about. The name I give it is dharma: the question of what each of us is required to do, in this particular moment, given who we are and what the situation demands. It is an ancient question. The answers will have to be new.

***

WHAT CIVILIZATIONAL TRANSITIONS ACTUALLY FEEL LIKE

We have the advantage and disadvantage of living inside the transition rather than observing it from a historical distance. The advantage is that our choices still matter — the infrastructure is not yet set, the institutions are still forming, the norms have not yet calcified into assumptions that feel as natural and inevitable as the air. The disadvantage is that we cannot see the shape of what we are inside. We experience it as a series of specific pressures, specific confusions, specific encounters with change — not as a unified narrative.

We are the participants, not the historians. We will not fully understand what we are living through until the generation after us tells us. But that does not mean we are helpless. The participants in every civilisational transition made choices that mattered — choices about what to build, what to protect, what norms to insist upon, what to refuse — and those choices shaped the narrative that the historians eventually assembled.

The people who understood, in the middle of any major information revolution, that new institutions would be needed — that the abundance of new material required new standards for evaluating it, new habits for engaging with it, new structures for deciding what to trust — were not trying to manage an outcome they understood. They were responding, with whatever wisdom they had, to specific pressures they were experiencing. The institutions that emerged were not designed by anyone. They accumulated through the choices of many people who were trying to make sense of a world that had changed faster than their inherited categories.

This is what we are doing. Whether we know it or not, we are building the institutions, the habits, the norms, and the vocabulary through which the next generation will relate to systems of collective memory that are more powerful than anything previously available. We are not doing this from a position of full knowledge, full consensus, or full control. We are doing it under conditions of uncertainty, disagreement, and speed that are challenging.

But we are doing it. The question is not whether the transition will happen — it is already happening, in millions of small encounters between human judgment and machine capability, in hospitals and law firms and classrooms and newsrooms and government offices across the world. The question is what kind of transition it will be. What norms will take hold. What accountability structures will emerge. What relationship between human agency and machine capability will become the default. These are not predetermined outcomes. They are choices in the process of being made.

That recognition — that we are in the middle of choices that will matter, and not at the beginning of a process that has not yet started or the end of one that has been decided — is where this book begins. The four movements that follow it are: shock, Fracture, Reckoning, and Choice; these are not stages that happen in sequence. They are dimensions of a single ongoing experience that most of us are living simultaneously. You may find yourself in different chapters on different days, in different professional contexts, in different conversations. That is as it should be. The experience is not uniform, and any account of it that pretends otherwise is describing something simpler than what we are actually living.

PART I

Shock

The world changed before most people noticed.

CHAPTER 1

The Day Time Collapsed

"What hath God wrought."

— *Samuel Morse, first telegraph transmission, 24 May 1844*

On the morning of May 24, 1844, a man named Samuel Morse sat in the chamber of the United States Supreme Court in Washington, D.C., and tapped out four words in a code of his own invention: "What hath God wrought."

The message travelled forty miles of copper wire to a receiving station in Baltimore, where his associate Alfred Vail decoded it and sent the same words back. The round trip took seconds. The two men were, at that moment, communicating faster than any two human beings had ever communicated across that distance in the entirety of recorded history.

The immediate public reaction was not purely celebratory. There was wonder, certainly — the demonstration drew crowds and the press reported it widely. But mixed into the wonder was a quality of unease that is hard to reconstruct from this distance. The telegraph violated something that people had assumed was simply a law of nature: that information moved at the speed of a physical carrier. A letter travelled at the speed of a horse or a ship. News of a battle arrived days or weeks after the battle ended. The world had been organised, for all of human history, around this constraint. Wars were won and lost by the speed of messengers. Prices at distant markets could diverge for months before correcting. Political decisions were made in the absence of relevant information simply because the information had not yet arrived.

One early editorial response captures the discomfort with particular clarity. "It is too fast for the truth," wrote a correspondent in a London newspaper in the months after the telegraph began operating commercially. The reporter was not being merely curmudgeonly. He was articulating something real: that the institutions of his world — the press, the courts, the markets, the governments — had been calibrated for a specific pace of information, and that a technology that violated that pace would require those institutions to change in ways that were not yet visible. He was right. It would take decades for those changes to work their way through every system that the telegraph touched. And some of them would prove more disruptive than anyone in 1844 had anticipated.

***

FORTY-SEVEN SECONDS

There is a particular kind of Tuesday morning that Raj knew better than most people. Not the crisis kind, where you arrive to find the office in controlled panic over something that happened overnight. Not the triumphant kind, where a project closes, and the team celebrates in the conference room. The Tuesday that Raj knew best was the quotidian kind: the kind where you have been doing this long enough that the rhythms are automatic, where you know what the day will ask of you before it asks, where your value is measured in the accumulated skill that produces, reliably and on schedule, what clients need.

That specific Tuesday, the office coffee machine was broken. A small thing. He had to use the pod machine in the corner of the kitchen, which produced coffee that tasted faintly of the plastic housing. He carried the cup to his desk, settled in, and opened his laptop to begin working on a strategic analysis he had promised a client by Friday.

The analysis required him to synthesise competitive intelligence from three industries, cross-reference it against macroeconomic trends, and frame the implications for a specific acquisition decision. It was the kind of work he had spent fifteen years becoming good at.

Instead of beginning the research process he would normally begin — the systematic reading, the note-taking, the gradual accumulation of a picture — he found himself, almost without deciding, typing the core question into one of the new AI systems he had been meaning to explore for months. He framed it the way he would frame a brief for a junior analyst, with context and constraints clearly stated. Then he waited.

Forty-seven seconds later, the screen began to fill.

It was not a rough draft but a structured analysis with an executive summary, a competitive landscape broken down by sector, a synthesis of the relevant macroeconomic trends, and a set of strategic implications that were organised around exactly the acquisition question he had specified. It cited reasoning rather than sources — a limitation he noted — but the reasoning was largely sound. He checked three of the factual claims against databases he had open in other tabs. Two were correct. One needed adjustment.

He stared at the screen longer than was probably rational. Not because something was wrong. Because nothing was wrong. The analysis was not perfect — it lacked the specific contextual judgment he would bring, the knowledge of this particular client's risk appetite, the understanding of a regulatory nuance that had come up in a conversation last month. Those gaps were real. But the structural architecture of the work? The synthesis that assembled the picture? That had been produced in less time than it had taken him to make and carry his mediocre cup of coffee.

He closed the laptop. He went back to the kitchen and poured the pod coffee down the sink and made tea instead — tea requiring more deliberate attention, which was what he wanted at that moment. He stood at the window while it steeped. The street below was full of the ordinary business of a Tuesday morning: people going where they were going, carrying what they were carrying, in the unhurried purposefulness of those who have somewhere to be.

The thought that arrived, and that he immediately disliked, was this: if the research and synthesis he had spent fifteen years becoming expert at could be produced in forty-seven seconds, what exactly was he being paid for? It was not, at its core, a financial question. It was a question about role, about what his position actually required of him now that the conditions around it had changed. It was the kind of question — though he would not have put it this way on a Tuesday morning with mediocre tea — that every generation eventually has to answer about itself: what does this moment actually need from me?

***

MEERA

That evening, at dinner, his wife Meera noticed something was different. She noticed it the way partners notice things — not through any single signal but through the accumulated understanding of sixteen years of watching someone's face across a table. She said nothing during the meal. Their daughter Nisha, nine years old and currently fascinated by the migratory patterns of Arctic terns, provided the conversational content. Raj listened, asked questions, ate his food, and performed the ordinariness of a weekday dinner with sufficient skill that most observers would have been convinced.

Meera was not most observers.

"You seem quiet tonight," she said when Nisha had gone to bed and they were clearing the table.

"Just tired," Raj said.

Meera looked at him for a moment — a look that did not so much challenge his answer as simply register that she had heard it. "That's not what tired looks like on you," she said, and went back to the kitchen.

She was right. It was not tiredness. He lay awake that night until nearly two in the morning, the ceiling of their bedroom a pale rectangle in the darkness, his mind running the same calculation repeatedly and arriving at the same uncomfortable place. The question was not whether the work could be done by such a system. He had seen that it could. The question was what that meant — for him, for his colleagues, for the fifteen junior analysts at his firm who were, right now, building their careers through the kind of research synthesis that the system had produced in forty-seven seconds.

Around two in the morning, he made a decision that would turn out to be one of the more consequential small decisions of his professional life: he decided not to dismiss what he had seen. He would not tell himself it was a party trick, a novelty, an impressive but ultimately superficial demonstration. He had seen enough of technology to know the difference between a novelty and an inflection. This was an inflection. What it inflected into remained inchoate — a shape he could not yet name, a rearrangement whose outlines were only beginning to emerge. But he knew that finding out was the most important professional project he had.

The next morning, he woke before his alarm and lay still in the early light, listening to the city begin. Meera was still asleep. He turned his head and looked at her — the particular way she slept, one hand under her cheek and thought about what she had said the night before. That's not what tired looks like on you. She had been right. And she had not pushed, had not demanded the explanation he wasn't ready to give. That was the particular gift of a long partnership: the capacity to register something important and wait for the other person to arrive at it.

He made coffee and sat with it at the kitchen table and spent the hour before the household woke up trying to think clearly about what he had seen. Not the forty-seven seconds specifically — that was already fading into the status of an example, a data point. The underlying question. What was the actual function of his work, stripped of the specific methods through which it had been delivered? What did clients actually need from him, when you removed the specific tasks that could now be done differently?

He had been in consulting long enough to know that this question — what is the actual function of what I do? — was always harder to answer than it appeared. It was harder because most professional work is performed through specific methods, and those methods over time become the work, in the practitioner's own understanding and in the client's. The method and the purpose fuse. The separation is uncomfortable because it reveals how much of what you do is contingent — dependent on the specific constraints that made a certain approach necessary — and how much is essential.

By seven o'clock, when Meera came downstairs, and Nisha followed shortly after, asking immediately about whether Arctic terns slept while flying (they did, apparently, half a brain at a time), Raj had reached a provisional answer: what clients actually needed from him was judgment, not information. They needed someone who understood their specific context, their specific risk tolerance, their specific institutional history, and could apply that understanding to whatever analytical picture was available. The analytical picture had just gotten faster to produce. The judgment that made the picture useful had not.

It was a provisional answer. It would take three years to test fully. But it was the right question, asked on the right morning, and that — he would later think — was most of what was required.

***

WHAT THE TELEGRAPH REALLY CHANGED

The telegraph did not merely make communication faster. That framing — faster communication — makes it sound like a quantitative improvement on what existed before, as if the telegraph were simply a very quick horse. What the telegraph actually did was change the structure of the world by breaking the link between information and physical movement. For all of human history, information had a body. It was carried by a person or inscribed on an object. The telegraph removed that body. Information became, for the first time, a pure signal —

able to move at speeds no physical carrier could match, across distances that would have required days or weeks.

The consequences cascaded. Financial markets, which had previously operated with information that lagged by days across cities, began to synchronize. The price of cotton in Liverpool and New York began to move together, because the arbitrage opportunities that had previously sustained the gap could no longer survive the speed of communication. Journalism transformed: the telegraph enabled the first wire services, the first nationally distributed news, the first sense that citizens in different cities were living through the same present moment. Military strategy changed: commanders could receive and send orders in real time across vast theaters of operation, which changed both what was possible and what was expected.

But something more fundamental changed too, something that is harder to name. The telegraph created, for the first time, a global nervous system — a network through which events in one part of the world could cause near-instantaneous reactions in another. The world became connected in a way that it had never been, and that connection created a new kind of vulnerability: what happened anywhere could affect everywhere. The interdependencies that the telegraph created were real gains. They were also new exposures to risk that the pre-telegraph world had been too slow to transmit.

This is the deeper pattern that matters, and the one that I keep returning to as I think about our current moment.

Transformative technologies do not merely change individual processes. They change the structure of what is possible — and in doing so, they change the structure of what is required. The world organised itself to take advantage of the telegraph, and in organising itself, it created obligations, expectations, and vulnerabilities that the pre-telegraph world could not have imagined. The people who understood that reorganisation earliest, who adapted their behaviour and their institutions to it while others were still assuming the old rules applied, shaped the world that everyone else eventually had to live in.

Raj had understood, lying awake at two in the morning, that he was at an equivalent moment. Not for the world; the world would figure this out on its own schedule, as it always does, through the aggregate of millions of individual encounters with a technology that changed what was possible. But for himself. He had been given, in forty-seven seconds, a glimpse of what the new structure of his profession might look like. What he chose to do with that glimpse was up to him.

***

THREE MONTHS LATER

Three months after the Tuesday with the broken coffee machine, Raj sat across from the same client whose acquisition analysis had been his project that day. The meeting had been called to review his firm's recommendation on the transaction — a recommendation that Raj had spent six weeks developing, using a combination of AI-assisted research and the kind of human judgment that required knowing the client, the industry, and the specific regulatory history that shaped this particular deal.

The client, a CFO named Deepa, had been in the industry for twenty years and had no patience for consultants who dressed up thin thinking in confident packaging, reviewed the presentation in her characteristic silence, flipping between pages, making small marks in the margins, asking no questions until she had seen everything.

"This section," she said finally, tapping a page that contained the synthesis of competitive intelligence. "This is unusually thorough. More thorough than usual." It was not quite a compliment. It was an observation offered with a question embedded in it.

"The research process has changed," Raj said carefully.

She looked at him. "Changed how?"

He thought for a moment, then decided to be direct. He told her. Not everything, not the forty-seven seconds, not the sleepless night, but the essential truth: that his firm was now using AI-assisted analysis for the research synthesis layer of client work, with human judgment applied to the contextual and strategic layers. That this allowed more thorough coverage of the competitive landscape. That the recommendation she was reading reflected both.

Deepa was quiet for several seconds. "And the judgment layer?" she said. "The part where you told me eighteen months ago not to do a deal that would have been a mistake. Is that still you?"

"Yes," Raj said. "That part hasn't changed."

She looked at the presentation for another moment. Then she said, "Good. That's what I'm paying for." She turned to the next page.

Raj drove home that evening thinking about what she had said. She had identified, with the perspicacity of someone who had spent twenty years paying for advice, exactly the line that the technology had drawn — between the synthesis that could be automated and the judgment that could not. She had not been threatened by the automation. She had been clarifying what she still needed from a human. The question that followed Raj home was whether he and his colleagues understood that distinction as clearly as she did.

***

THE SECTORS THAT CHANGED FASTEST

The compression happened unevenly. Some sectors moved into the new configuration quickly; others are still finding their way. The pattern does not follow the lines that most people expected. It is not, primarily, the most information-intensive sectors that have changed fastest. It is the sectors where the barriers to adoption were lowest, where the gap between "this could change how we work" and "this is now how we work" required the fewest institutional gatekeepers.

In consulting, the change came quickly because the product was always information and analysis, and the value chain was already lean and a small number of highly skilled people producing work that had always been synthesised from large bodies of information. When the synthesis layer became dramatically cheaper, the business model had to change dramatically, and it did, faster than most firms' strategic planning cycles had anticipated.

In law, the change came more slowly, partly because of regulatory structures and professional liability frameworks that created friction, and partly because legal judgment is more deeply embedded in relational and contextual factors that resist automation. But it came. The junior associate reviewing discovery documents, the paralegal summarizing deposition transcripts, the first-pass research on a novel legal question — these functions did not disappear, but they are now done differently, faster, and with different economics than they were a decade ago.

In medicine, the change is happening in a more complicated way, because medicine carries the highest stakes for error and the strongest existing regulatory frameworks. The change is visible in radiology, in pathology, in monitoring, in administrative functions. It is slower in the domains of clinical judgment where error is more likely to be caught, and its consequences are most severe. But it is happening, and the physicians who understand what is changing and what is not are better positioned than those who either embrace everything uncritically or resist everything reflexively.

In education, the change is just beginning in institutional terms, though individual teachers and students have been navigating it for years. The institutional response is lagging, as it always does, behind the lived reality of students who are using these tools whether or not their schools have policies about them, and behind the reality of teachers who are finding that the work they were trained to do — the delivery of content — is a smaller part of their value than it used to be, while the work they were not specifically trained for — the facilitation of genuine inquiry — is increasingly what matters.

What these patterns share is that the change is not primarily about what the technology can do. It is about what changes when organisations and individuals decide to use it differently — when the question shifts from "can we use this?" to "how do we use this in ways that actually serve the purposes we care about?" That second question is harder, more institutional, and more human than the first. It is also the one that most determines outcomes.

WHAT THE COMPRESSION ACTUALLY MEANT

Raj's forty-seven seconds is a personal data point, not a general truth. But the phenomenon it represents is general, and it has a structure that is worth examining carefully before moving on.

What was compressed was not time in the abstract. It was the time required for a specific cognitive operation: the synthesis of a large body of heterogeneous information into a structured analytical product. This operation had previously required a certain number of skilled hours, which is to say a certain amount of human cognitive effort, which is to say a certain cost, which is to say a certain institutional infrastructure — analysts, research teams, databases, methodologies, billing structures, management layers — organised around the assumption that the operation was expensive.

When the operation became cheap, all of those downstream implications shifted. Not immediately — institutional inertia is real, and the adaptation of pricing structures and organisational forms to changed economics takes time. But directionally: the value of the infrastructure built around expensive synthesis was now a question, not an assumption, and that question would have to be answered.

The telegraph compression worked differently in detail but identically in structure. When Morse's first message moved from Baltimore to Washington in May 1844 — "What hath God wrought" — it did not merely demonstrate that communication could be fast. It demonstrated that communication could be fast over distances that previously made it slow. The implications were commercial: cotton prices in New Orleans could now inform trading decisions in New York before the ship that carried the cotton had arrived. The implications were political: a president could communicate with a general in the field faster than the general's own dispatches could return. The implications were social: what had been local news became national news, and what had been national news became global, and the meaning of "knowing what was happening" changed irrevocably.

None of these implications were obvious to the people who first sent messages over the telegraph wire. They understood the technology. They did not fully understand what they had made. The institutions that adapted fastest to the telegraph's implications were not the ones that understood it best in the abstract. They were the ones that thought hardest about what the specific operation it had made cheap — rapid long-distance communication — meant for their specific domain, and then reorganised themselves around that understanding.

This is what Raj was beginning to do, in the weeks after his Tuesday, more instinctively than analytically. He was asking not what AI could do in general but what the specific operation it had made cheap — synthesis of large information bodies — meant for the specific domain he occupied. The answer he was working toward was not comfortable. It pointed at a significant reorganisation of what his work was actually for, and what made it valuable, and what clients like Deepa were paying for. But it was an answer or at least, the beginning of one, and the beginning of an answer is enormously more useful than a refusal to ask the question.

***

WHAT DID NOT CHANGE

There is a mistake that is easy to make when confronting a disruption of this kind: concluding that because something has changed significantly, everything has changed. This is not true, and believing it produces a kind of paralysis that is itself costly.

What did not change, on Raj's Tuesday, was the nature of the problem his clients needed to solve. The CFO considering an acquisition still needed to understand whether the target was worth acquiring, at what price, under what terms, and with what assumptions about what would happen afterward. The system could now do the initial synthesis faster. The CFO's need — to make a sound decision under uncertainty, in the context of a specific company with a specific history and specific strategic goals — was identical to what it had been before.

What did not change was the value of understanding the client. Deepa had been in the industry for twenty years. What she had told Raj, with the precision of someone who had spent decades paying for advice, was that the thing she valued — the thing she was actually paying for — was the judgment layer. The specific knowledge of her situation, her risk tolerance, her strategic context. No system had that. No system would have that. It lived in the relationship, in the accumulated understanding built through years of working together, in the particular texture of her professional history that only someone who had engaged with it carefully could know.

What did not change was the difficulty of doing this work well. If anything, the work became harder — not because the tools made it harder but because the tools changed what "doing it well" meant. Doing it well now required maintaining genuine analytical capability alongside the efficient use of automated tools, remaining able to distinguish between the system's reliable outputs and its errors, and preserving the contextual judgment that no tool could replace. This was more demanding, in some ways, than the previous version of the work. It required more metacognitive sophistication — knowing what you know, and what you're relying on to know it, and what would happen to your judgment if the tool were unavailable.

Raj would spend the next year learning to articulate this. Learning to explain to clients what had changed and what had not. Learning to demonstrate, in the quality of his judgment, that the reorganisation of his practice was not a diminishment of it. Learning to value in himself what Deepa had already identified as valuable: not the synthesis, which could now be done quickly, but the judgment about what the synthesis meant for this particular decision, at this particular moment, with these particular stakes.

***

What changed on Raj's Tuesday was not the nature of his expertise. It was the location of memory. The synthesis that had lived inside him the accumulated pattern-recognition of two decades of client work, now had a technological parallel that could be accessed by anyone with a question. The container had externalised. The judgment had not moved with it. That was both the disruption and the opportunity.

The pattern Raj was navigating had, by that point, already been documented in aggregate. Studies of GitHub Copilot — an AI code-completion assistant adopted by hundreds of thousands of developers within months of its launch — showed something that would have felt familiar to him: experienced developers completing programming tasks up to 55% faster. The time compression was real and measurable. But the same research found that developers who relied heavily on AI-generated code were introducing security vulnerabilities at higher rates than peers who worked without the assistance. The tool accelerated everyone. The judgment about when to accept a suggestion and when to override it — about when the fast answer was also the right answer — was not equally distributed. Speed had compressed. Discernment had not followed automatically. The most valuable skill in the new environment was not facility with the tool. It was knowing what the tool was likely to get wrong.

The question was never whether the tools would change things. Every tool changes things. The question was whether the people using the tools, and the people affected by them, would understand the change clearly enough to navigate it — or whether they would spend years performing the old work in the new world, wondering why the rewards no longer matched the effort.

Raj had been given an early glimpse. He intended to use it.

CHAPTER 2

Memory Became External

"Writing creates forgetfulness in the learners' souls, because they will not use their memories; they will trust to the external written characters and not remember of themselves."

— Plato, Phaedrus, c. 370 BC (words attributed to Socrates)

Around 370 BC, Plato wrote a dialogue called Phaedrus, in which Socrates tells a story that is worth sitting with carefully. Socrates describes a meeting between the Egyptian god Thoth — the inventor of writing — and the king Thamus. Thoth presents his invention with pride: writing, he argues, is a remedy for the forgetfulness of human minds. People will be able to preserve their knowledge, to recall things they would otherwise lose.

Thamus disagrees, emphatically. "You who are the father of writing," the king says, "have in your fondness for it attributed to it a quality which it cannot have; for this discovery of yours will create forgetfulness in the learners' souls, because they will not use their memories; they will trust to the external written characters and not remember of themselves." Writing, Thamus argues, is not a supplement to memory. It is a replacement for it. And a replacement that produces the illusion of knowledge without its substance: people will "have read many things and have learned nothing," seeming wise when they are merely informed.

It is worth noting that we know this story because Plato wrote it down. And Plato's written account survived because copies were made and preserved. The warning against the dangers of writing was itself preserved through writing. This irony is not accidental. It is the condition of every technological transition: we cannot avoid using the tool to think about the tool, because the tool has already changed what thinking means.

***

THE HOSPITAL AT 3:47 AM

Maya had not slept properly in nine days when the patient arrived. This was not unusual for someone in her second year of residency — sleep deprivation was so structurally embedded in medical training that she had stopped noticing it the way you stop noticing background noise. She noticed it only when something else forced the recognition: a stumble on a staircase, a word she could not retrieve, the moment in a corridor when she stood with her hand on a doorknob for three seconds, having forgotten why she was there.

The patient was a man named Deepak, fifty-eight years old, a construction site supervisor who had come in through the emergency department at 3:47 in the morning with a complaint of headache and mild confusion. His wife had brought him, alarmed enough to come at that hour but not alarmed enough to call an ambulance. She sat in the waiting area in the particular posture of someone who has been sitting in waiting areas for hours: not quite awake, not quite at rest, her handbag in her lap and a cold cup of tea on the chair beside her.

Maya took Deepak's history. He had been having headaches for three days — moderate, mostly in the mornings, resolving by noon. He had attributed them to the dust on the construction site and had not gone to a doctor. His wife had noticed the confusion only that evening, when he had twice called her by the wrong name — his sister's name, she said, a detail that had frightened her more than the headaches.

Maya examined him. She ordered a basic blood panel. She ran through the differential in her head: tension headache, migraine, hypertension, early infection. Subdural hematoma was on the list but ranked lower — he had no reported head injury, no anticoagulant use, no obvious fall risk. She was thirty-two hours into a shift, and she knew that at thirty-two hours her cognitive hierarchy was not fully reliable, but she had no way to step outside herself to check it.

She stood in the corridor outside Deepak's room — fluorescent lights, the particular quality of hospital quiet at 4 AM, the smell of industrial cleaning products and something underneath that you learned, after enough time, not to identify. She looked at the chart in her hand and then, almost without deciding to, she opened the cognitive diagnostic support system her hospital had integrated into its workflow six months earlier.

She entered his age, his presenting symptoms, the timeline, the details his wife had provided about the wrong-name confusion. She hit submit. The system's response arrived in seconds. It offered a ranked differential diagnosis with probability weightings and a specific note at the top: "Bilateral subdural hematoma should be prioritised for imaging given symptom constellation and age profile. Recommends urgent CT without contrast."

She stared at the screen. Then she looked at the door to Deepak's room. Then she looked at the screen again.

The system had ranked subdural hematoma first. She had ranked it third. Not because she had missed it — it was on her list. Because something in the weighting of his presentation had led her to assign it less urgency than the system had assigned it, and she could not, in that moment, fully identify why. The wrong-name confusion. The morning-specific timing. The age profile cross-referenced against a pattern she did not consciously have access to but that the system had derived from its training on millions of patient presentations.

She ordered the CT.

Her attending physician, Dr. Krishnamurthy, found her in the corridor twenty minutes later, reviewing the scan results. He was a small, precise man who had been practicing medicine for thirty years and who expressed most of his opinions through the angle at which he tilted his head when looking at something.

He looked at the scan. He tilted his head. "Good catch," he said.

"It got there before I did," Maya said.

He looked at her. "It got there before you did," he said. Not an accusation. An observation. "How?"

"It had patterns from twenty million patients to learn from," Maya said. "I've had four hundred."

He was quiet for a moment. "That's the right way to think about it," he said. Then: "Order the occupational exposure workup too. Dust inhalation chronic can affect vasculature." He walked away.

The system had not replaced her clinical judgment. It had not made the diagnosis. It had surfaced a possibility that she might have reached herself, given more time and less fatigue. But it had reached it faster, and with a weighting that was, in this case, more accurate than her own. Those facts sat beside each other in her mind with a weight she did not yet know what to do with.

***

THE COMMUTE HOME

She rode the subway home at half past five in the morning. The train was mostly empty at that hour — a few nightshift workers, a young man asleep against the window with his mouth open, a woman in running clothes who had gotten on at the last stop and was studying something on her phone with the particular intensity of someone reading an important message. Maya found a seat and looked at her own hands for a while.

Deepak was in imaging. His wife was asleep in the waiting room, finally, her cold tea replaced by a warm one that someone had left for her. The CT had confirmed bilateral subdural haematomas — small, but there, and requiring monitoring. He would be admitted. He was not in immediate danger. He would, with a high degree of probability, go home to his family.

She thought about the system. About the twenty million patients it had learned from. About the four hundred she had seen. About the fact that those numbers were not a permanent ratio — she would see more patients, her experience would grow, her pattern recognition would deepen. But the system's training data would also grow. The gap between twenty million and four hundred would not close; it would simply move to a different scale.

She thought about Thamus's objection to writing. Writing creates forgetfulness in the learners' souls, because they will not use their memories. Was that what was happening? Was she in training to become a doctor who trusted external memory more than she trusted her own developing judgment? Was that a problem?

She was still thinking about this when she reached her stop. The morning was just beginning — a gray, slightly luminous morning that smelled of rain that had fallen overnight and pavement warming in the early light. She walked the three blocks to her apartment and let herself in and stood in the kitchen for a moment, too tired to sleep properly but too aware of what she needed to do that she couldn't simply lie down.

She made tea the way her mother had taught her — loose leaf, steeped for exactly four minutes, no longer or it became bitter. She sat with it at the kitchen table and wrote a few notes about the night in the journal she had been keeping since her first year of residency. Not clinical notes — those were in the system. Personal notes. What she had been thinking, what she had been uncertain about, what she had learned.

She wrote: "The system was right. I was less right. This is not a problem I know how to frame yet."

***

SOCRATES WAS RIGHT AND WRONG

The history of human cognition is a history of externalization. We have always offloaded portions of our thinking onto tools and environments. The knot tied in a handkerchief to remember an errand. The shopping list. The calendar. The filing system. The spreadsheet. Each of these is an external memory — a system outside the brain that takes on some of the cognitive work the brain would otherwise have to do.

The philosopher Andy Clark coined the term "extended mind" to describe this phenomenon — the idea that human cognition is not confined to the brain but routinely extends into notebooks, smartphones, the layout of desks, the design of cities. When you can't remember a phone number because it's stored in your contacts, your mind is, in Clark's framework, genuinely extended into your phone. The boundary between the self and the tool has become genuinely porous.

Socrates, through Thamus, was worried about this extension. If you write things down, you will not remember them yourself. You will become dependent on the external record. Your internal memory will atrophy from disuse, and what you will have in its place is not knowledge but access to knowledge — a very different thing, and in his view, an inferior one. Real wisdom, for Socrates, required that knowledge be genuinely incorporated — digested, internalized, available to the mind without external prompting.

He was right about the risk, and he was wrong about the conclusion. Writing did change what people needed to remember. It did create a kind of dependence — or rather, a kind of distributed cognition in which some things were held internally, and others were held externally. But this did not produce people who were less capable of wisdom. It produced people who could build on the written record in ways that purely oral cultures could not. It produced Euclid, whose geometric proofs depended on being able to write them down precisely enough that others could follow and extend them. It produced Aristotle, who systematized knowledge in ways that required the ability to organize and compare across texts. It produced science, which is built on the assumption that findings can be written down, reproduced, and revised.

What writing changed was not whether people could think. It was what they needed to think about — and what they could think about as a result. The externalization of memory freed cognitive resources for other things. It allowed civilisation to become what it now so evidently is: a palimpsest — each generation writing its understanding onto the record of the last, building upward without having to begin again from silence, with the traces of earlier layers still legible beneath the new.

What these new systems externalize is something more ambitious: not just storage, not just organisation, but the synthesis of information into understanding. Not storage of the record, but the beginning of the analysis of the record. If that externalization follows the same pattern as every previous externalization — and history suggests it will — it will free human cognitive resources for something that the new tools cannot do. The question, urgently present, is what that something is.

***

WHAT GETS FREED

In medicine, the answer is beginning to come into focus. The functions that AI diagnostic systems are most demonstrably improving are the functions that require pattern-matching across large populations: the recognition of statistical regularities in how symptoms cluster, the identification of correlations between presentations and outcomes, the flagging of cases whose profiles match historical patterns of serious but underdiagnosed conditions. These are functions that human physicians were always performing — but performing with the cognitive overhead of building the statistical model from scratch, inside their own heads, from their own limited exposure to patients.

When those functions are better handled by external systems, what gets freed — in principle — is the physician's attention for what external systems cannot do. The patient who is in the room, who is frightened, who is telling you something about their life as well as their symptoms, who has a history and a family and a set of concerns that are not in any dataset. The judgment about what kind of intervention is appropriate given not just the diagnosis but the specific person who has it. The relationship between clinician and patient that makes adherence to treatment possible and that no algorithm can substitute for. These are not peripheral functions of medicine. They are, in many practitioners' view, its core.

The same pattern appears in law. The AI-assisted legal research systems that are now in regular use at most major firms have dramatically reduced the time required for the kind of comprehensive case law review that once consumed a significant portion of junior associates' working hours. What this frees, at its best, is time for the work that legal practice exists to do: understanding what a client actually needs, developing a strategic approach to their situation, building the relationships that allow effective advocacy, and exercising the judgment about when to fight and when to settle that no research system can provide.

In education, the possibility is analogous. Teaching has always contained two distinct functions that have been awkwardly bundled together: the transmission of information, and the facilitation of genuine understanding. These are different activities requiring different skills and producing different outcomes. The transmission function has always been constrained by time and access — there are only so many hours in a classroom, only so many students a teacher can reach effectively.

AI systems are already demonstrably improving access to the transmission function: personalised practice problems, adaptive explanation of concepts, immediate feedback on exercises. If that function becomes sufficiently well-served by technology, what gets freed is teacher attention for the function that the technology cannot substitute: the cultivation of genuine understanding, the navigation of confusion, the specific and irreplaceable work of being present with a student at the moment when something clicks.

None of this is guaranteed. Freed time and attention can be refilled by administrative burden, by additional volume of work, by new demands that colonize the space that technology opened. The history of labour-saving technology is partly a history of time savings being captured by productivity demands rather than by quality improvements. Whether the cognitive freed-up by AI systems goes toward the irreducibly human work that matters, or simply gets absorbed into doing more of the same work faster, is not a technological question. It is a design question — about how organisations and institutions choose to use the capacity that the technology creates. Those choices are being made now, mostly without adequate reflection on what is actually at stake.

***

THE INFRASTRUCTURE OF KNOWING

Six months after the 3:47 AM encounter with the diagnostic system's correct prediction, Maya had a case that went the other way. A patient presented with symptoms that the system classified with high confidence as a medication reaction. Maya had been increasingly trusting the system's high-confidence outputs; they had been right often enough that she had raised her threshold for independent second-guessing. She did not order the additional imaging that her own clinical instinct, quieter now than it had been, would have suggested.

The patient was transferred to another service two days later, and the imaging that service ordered revealed a condition that the medication reaction diagnosis had obscured. The condition was treatable. The patient was not harmed in any permanent way. But the delay mattered, and the delay had a cause that Maya could identify with uncomfortable clarity.

She wrote about this in her journal. Not in the way she would have written about it in her first year — anxious, catastrophizing, afraid she was not suited for medicine. In the way she had learned to write about errors that were instructive: what she had been thinking, what information had been available to her, what she had decided and why, what she had missed and why. She was not flagellating herself. She was auditing the failure.

What the audit revealed was not a single decision error but a pattern: she had been allowing the system's confidence scores to substitute for her own clinical assessment in a way she had not explicitly decided to do. The substitution had happened gradually, through the accumulation of individual interactions where the system had been right and she had been wrong, and where the lesson she had drawn — unconsciously — was that the system's confidence was more reliable than her intuition. This was, in most cases, true. In this case, it had failed.

She brought the case to Anand the following week. He was not judgmental. He was curious. "The question," he said, "is whether this is a calibration error or a framework error. A calibration error is: you were trusting the system too much in this specific kind of case, and now you know that and you'll adjust. A framework error is: you've been thinking about the trust question wrong in some more general way, and fixing it requires rethinking the framework."

"Which do you think it is?" Maya asked.

"I think it's a framework error," he said carefully. "I think you've been thinking of the system's confidence as a substitute for your clinical model rather than as an input to it. Those are different relationships with the same tool. And the one you were using is the more dangerous one."

She thought about this for a long time. It was not a comfortable conclusion. The framework error was harder to fix than the calibration error — it required not just adjusting a threshold but reconstructing a habit of mind that had developed over two years of practice. It required deliberately re-engaging her own clinical model in cases where she had been allowing the system's output to preempt it.

She started doing this. It was slower. It was sometimes redundant — her clinical model and the system's output agreed, and she had spent additional cognitive effort to confirm what was already confirmed. But occasionally, perhaps once a month, she found a divergence that mattered: a case where her reading of the patient in front of her produced a different hypothesis than the system's reading of the data, and where pursuing her hypothesis added something. Not always a dramatic finding. Sometimes just a clarification. But the capacity to find that divergence — to maintain the internal model that could be compared against the external one — was exactly what the system could not replace and what the previous two years of practice had almost allowed her to let atrophy.

Maya spent the next three weeks thinking about the question she had written in her journal. She talked about it with colleagues. Most of them, she found, had already made a kind of provisional peace with the system's presence — they used it when it was useful, overrode it when their judgment differed, and had not particularly examined the epistemological implications of doing either.

A few were actively resistant to it, on grounds that ranged from principled concern about deskilling to something that looked more like professional pride. A very small number had thought carefully about what it meant.

One of them was a fourth-year resident named Anand, who had done his undergraduate work in philosophy before pivoting to medicine. He and Maya had dinner one evening, and the conversation found its way, as it often did with Anand, to the fundamental question.

"The thing Krishnamurthy said," Maya told him. "It got there before you did. I keep coming back to that."

"What's the question you're actually asking?" Anand said.

"Whether I should trust my judgment or the system's. In cases where they differ."

Anand was quiet for a moment. "That's the wrong question," he said. "Or at least, it's not quite the right question. The right question is: what did the system see that you didn't? If you can answer that — if you can understand the mechanism of the discrepancy — then you're doing medicine. If you can't, if you're just deferring to whichever authority feels more credible in the moment and hoping you've chosen well, then something has gone wrong."

Maya thought about this for a long time. "And if I never understand the mechanism? If the system operates in ways that I can't fully audit or replicate?"

"Then you understand your dependency," Anand said. "Which is different from having none. And that understanding — knowing what you rely on and why and what happens if it fails — is itself a form of knowledge worth having."

She went home that evening and added to her journal: "The goal is not to not depend on external memory. The goal is to know what you're depending on, and to keep the judgment that external memory can't replace."

***

THE QUESTION OF DEPENDENCY

A year into her residency, Maya had a conversation with a senior physician — a cardiologist named Dr. Krishnamurthy, whose reputation in the hospital was built on diagnostic instincts developed over thirty years of practice — that she found herself returning to often in the months that followed.

He had pulled her aside after she correctly identified a subtle arrhythmia that the monitoring system had flagged but that she had initially dismissed as artifact before the system's persistence prompted her to look again. "You trusted the machine this time," he said. It was not an accusation. It was an observation.

"It was right," she said. "I was going to miss it."

He nodded slowly. "It will be right more often than it is wrong," he said. "That is the nature of systems trained on large populations. They are very good at what is probable. They are less reliable on what is unusual." He paused. "The difficult part of this work is that the unusual cases are often the ones that matter most. The cases that don't fit the pattern. The presentations that shouldn't be what they are but are. Those are the cases that will kill a patient if the system gets them wrong and you are not present enough to catch it."

Maya thought about this for a long time. The cardiologist was not arguing against using the monitoring system. He was arguing for a particular kind of attentiveness in using it: not the passive trust of someone who has outsourced the thinking, but the active engagement of someone who uses the tool's output as one input among several, who maintains enough independent clinical judgment to notice when the tool is being wrong in an important way.

This is, she eventually came to understand, the specific cognitive posture that every generation of knowledge workers must develop anew with every new generation of cognitive tools. Socrates's students had to learn to use writing without losing the capacity for memory and argument. Scholars who gained access to printing had to learn to read critically, not just reverently. The first generation of researchers who had access to electronic databases had to learn to search effectively without losing the deeper contextual knowledge that allowed them to evaluate what they found. Maya's generation had to learn to use diagnostic AI without losing the clinical judgment that gave the AI's output its appropriate weight.

The dependency that Socrates feared was real. The conclusion he drew from it was wrong. Writing did create dependency — you could no longer practice certain skills of oral memory if you had access to written records. But the dependency was generative rather than merely corrosive. It freed cognitive resources for other things. The person who could write did not become cognitively weaker. They became cognitively different — capable of things that no purely oral culture had managed.

What Maya was navigating was the analogous transition for her generation. The dependency she was developing on diagnostic AI was real. The question was whether it was generative or corrosive — whether it was freeing her to do things that required the clinical judgment the system could not replace, or whether it was replacing that judgment without developing anything in its place. The answer depended on choices she was making and would continue to make: about what she paid attention to, about how she engaged with the system's outputs, about whether she maintained the internal clinical model that would allow her to catch the cases where the system was being importantly wrong.

These choices were not dramatic. They were made in small moments — the decision to think through a differential diagnosis before checking the system's suggestion, the sedulous habit of asking what else the presentation could be rather than accepting the highest-probability answer, the practice of writing down her own initial impression before reviewing the system's output. Tiny adjustments in daily practice. The accumulation of those adjustments, over years, was what would determine whether she became the kind of physician that Dr. Krishnamurthy was describing: present enough to catch what the system missed, while skilled enough to use what the system offered.

***

The challenge Maya was sensing had already manifested at institutional scale. In 2013, the MD Anderson Cancer Center entered an ambitious partnership with IBM to deploy an AI system for oncology — a programme aimed at recommending cancer treatments based on the accumulated evidence in the medical literature. The project ran for four years and cost nearly $62 million before it was discontinued in 2017.

The internal audit identified a central problem: the system had been trained predominantly on hypothetical patient cases prepared by physicians, not on the records of actual patients who had been treated and whose outcomes were known. It had absorbed the record. It had not absorbed what the record meant in practice — the specific complexity of actual clinical presentations, the cases that didn't fit the textbook, the judgment about when to follow the protocol and when to deviate from it. The vast external memory, it turned out, was not a substitute for the clinical experience that knew what to do with it. Maya's journal entry could have been the audit's conclusion: the goal is not to not depend on external memory. The goal is to know what you're depending on, and to keep the judgment that external memory cannot replace.

Thamus was worried about writing. We are navigating the final stage of the externalisation he feared: a system that not only stores the record but synthesises it on demand. The question he raised — what remains in the human mind when memory moves outside it? — is the animating question of this entire book. We did not build artificial intelligence. We built civilisation's external memory. What we do with what remains inside us is what everything that follows is about.

What Thamus feared was not memory loss. What he feared was the displacement of judgment by information — the confusion of having read something with having understood it. His king's worry was prophetic, and it remains the right worry. Not because external memory is dangerous. Because every generation that acquires powerful external memory must learn, anew, the difference between the record and the wisdom that the record is supposed to serve.

CHAPTER 3

The Early Movers Rewrite Reality

"Printing, gunpowder, and the compass — these three have changed the whole face and state of things throughout the world."

— Francis Bacon, Novum Organum, 1620

In the early 1450s, a goldsmith from Mainz named Johannes Gutenberg was working in a workshop that smelled of lead and linseed oil and the particular metallic warmth of a casting process that had never been applied to this purpose before. He was trying to solve a mechanical problem: how to produce letterforms that could be assembled into text, pressed onto paper reliably and repeatedly, and then reassembled into different text for the next job. The problem was harder than it sounds. Letters vary in width. The pressure required to transfer ink from metal to paper without smearing had to be precisely calibrated. The oil-based ink he needed had to be viscous enough to adhere to metal but fluid enough to transfer cleanly.

He solved these problems over years of iteration — developing a hand mould that could cast individual letters with mechanical precision, perfecting an oil-based ink, adapting the screw press from winemaking into something capable of applying even, controlled pressure across a full page. When the pieces came together, what he had built was not merely a faster way to copy books. It was the first system in the European world capable of producing identical text at scale — text in which every copy was precisely the same as every other, producible at a cost that made books accessible to people who had never been able to afford them.

The first major product of this system was a Bible. The Gutenberg Bible, completed around 1455, was printed in an edition of approximately 180 copies — a number that seems small by modern standards but was, at the time, comparable to the entire annual output of a scriptorium staffed with professional copyists. Each copy was identical. Each copy cost a fraction of what a hand-copied Bible would have cost. And each copy could be produced again, and again, and again, as long as the type held and the press operated.

The early printers — those who grasped, in those first years, what the press actually meant — did not merely become wealthy. They became, for a period of perhaps twenty to thirty years, the primary architects of European intellectual culture. They decided what was printed. They decided what was available. They determined which ancient texts would be rediscovered and which would remain inaccessible. They chose the languages in which texts would appear, and those choices shaped which vernacular languages would develop literary traditions and which would remain primarily spoken. The printers of the late fifteenth and early sixteenth centuries made decisions whose consequences lasted for centuries, not because they were uniquely wise, but because they moved first in a moment when the power to shape the information environment was briefly concentrated in the hands of those who understood the new technology.

Gutenberg himself did not share in this prosperity. He was taken to court by his primary financial backer, Johann Fust, who won the lawsuit in 1455 and took possession of the press, the type, and the completed Bible. Gutenberg spent his final years in financial difficulty, receiving a modest pension from the Archbishop of Mainz in 1465, and died in 1468 — recognised in his city but never wealthy, never fully compensated for what he had unleashed. The technology he had created reshaped civilisation. The civilisation it reshaped did not adequately reward its creator.

This detail is not a footnote. It is the part of the Gutenberg story that the contemporary moment most needs to sit with. The person who builds the transformative technology does not necessarily control what it becomes. The inventor and the entrepreneur and the institution that eventually shapes the technology into permanent infrastructure are often different people, and the inventor is often the one with the least durable claim on what they created. Gutenberg built the press. The publishing houses that followed — Aldus Manutius in Venice, Christoph Plantin in Antwerp, the great printers of Paris and London — built the industry. The people who built the industry are the ones who shaped what was printed. Gutenberg shaped what was possible. Possibility and actuality are different, and the gap between them is where power lives.

The equivalent question for the current moment is not only who will build the AI systems that reshape the world. It is who will build the institutions around those systems — who will govern access, set the terms of use, determine what gets trained and what gets filtered, decide whose interests the systems will be optimised for when the interests of different groups conflict. These institutional choices are the equivalent of the publishing houses that followed Gutenberg. They will determine what the technology actually does in the world, long after the technical innovations that made it possible have become standard and widespread.

***

TWO HOSPITALS

The same pattern reasserts itself whenever a new information technology arrives — and it is reasserting itself now, with a speed and comprehensiveness that exceeds any previous precedent. The organisations that are moving first are not simply gaining an efficiency advantage. They are acquiring the capacity to rewrite the assumptions that everyone else will eventually have to navigate.

People like to believe that transformative technologies arrive equally — that everyone has access at the same moment, and that the benefits therefore distribute democratically. This comforting idea is consistently contradicted by the historical record. The technology was available, in principle, to anyone who could afford it. In practice, the institutions that moved first established positions that took generations to dislodge. Everyone eventually got access. Not everyone got equal power over what was built with it.

Two hospitals. Let us be specific. Two hospitals in the same city, serving populations of similar size, with similar patient demographics and similar baseline resources. Both had access to the same AI-assisted diagnostic and operational systems. Both introduced those systems in the same twelve-month period. The difference was entirely in how they introduced them.

The first hospital — call it Hospital A — approached the technology as an efficiency improvement. Physicians used the diagnostic system the way they had used reference databases before it: as a tool to consult when uncertain, a supplement to existing workflows. Training was minimal, framed as technical onboarding. The governance remained unchanged. The system was layered onto existing practice without examining whether existing practice was optimal.

The second hospital — Hospital B — asked an uncomfortable question at the outset: not "how can we use this technology to do what we already do more efficiently?" but "if we could design our clinical workflows from scratch, knowing that this capability exists, what would we build?" The question required difficult conversations. It required acknowledging that some existing processes had been designed around constraints that no longer applied. It required physicians to be willing to see their workflows not as expressions of clinical wisdom but as historical artifacts, products of what was possible before, capable of being improved.

The governance process was harder. Some senior physicians felt threatened. The conversation surfaced tensions between departments that had existed for years but had been manageable within the existing structure. There were three months of meetings that felt, to many participants, more like therapy sessions than strategic planning.

At the end of those three months, Hospital B had something Hospital A did not: a coherent theory of what the technology was for, how it connected to their clinical mission, and how they would measure whether it was actually improving patient outcomes. They had also identified three specific workflow redesigns that their physicians were willing to commit to, knowing that the system's capabilities made those redesigns viable.

The difference became visible two years later. Hospital B's diagnostic accuracy on the category of presentations where the system had been integrated had improved by a statistically significant margin. Hospital A's had improved modestly — the system helped at the margins where it was consulted — but the structure of care had not changed. Hospital B's physicians were operating from a different epistemological position: they trusted the system in specific, well-defined ways, overrode it in specific, well-defined ways, and had a shared language for discussing the cases where human judgment and system output diverged.

Hospital A's physicians used the same tool. They got substantially different results. The difference was not the technology. It was the willingness to ask the harder question first.

The same dynamic played out at civilisational speed in 2020, when Moderna became one of the first companies to file an Investigational New Drug application after the COVID-19 genome was sequenced. The company had used AI-assisted tools to design the mRNA sequence for its vaccine candidate in roughly two days. The clinical trials took another year. The regulatory approval took months after that. The technology was fast; the institutional machinery around it moved at its own pace. But the early start that AI-assisted design enabled mattered enormously — not because it produced a better vaccine on the first try, but because it gave Moderna the runway to run the trials and accumulate the evidence that the slower-moving institutions required. Early movers don't always win. They get to play the game on better terms.

***

THE PSYCHOLOGY OF THE EARLY MOVER

Early adoption of a transformative technology is not primarily a technical act. It is a psychological one. It requires the willingness to accept that your current expertise — which you have spent years, sometimes decades, building — may be organised around constraints that are about to become obsolete. This is not a comfortable acceptance to make. Expertise is not merely skill. It is identity, investment, social position, the basis of professional relationships and institutional standing.

The early movers in every technological transition share a particular quality: they are able to disaggregate their identity from their current methods. They can say: what I am good at is the underlying problem — the clinical outcome, the analytical insight, the well-designed building — and not the specific method I have been using to pursue it. The specific method is contingent. The underlying problem is not.

This is difficult. It is made more difficult by the fact that the people who most need to make this disaggregation are often those who have the most invested in the current methods — the most experienced, the most credentialed, the most professionally embedded in the existing system. The junior resident can adapt more easily than the senior physician, not because she is smarter, but because she has less identity invested in the way things have been done. The new analyst can adapt more easily than the partner with thirty years of practice, for the same reason.

This creates a structural tension in every organisation navigating a major technological transition: the people with the most institutional authority tend to be the ones with the most resistance to the change, while the people with the least resistance tend to have the least authority. The organisations that navigate this transition best are the ones that find ways to use the experience and authority of the senior people while not allowing that authority to veto the adaptation that survival requires.

The institutions that adapted earliest set the terms that everyone else eventually had to navigate. The ones that moved slowly found themselves adapting to terms they had not chosen, in a configuration they had not designed, at a disadvantage they might have avoided. The printing press created this dynamic in the fifteenth century. Every major information technology since has created it again. We are in the middle of creating it again now.

What the early movers were actually competing to control was not the technology but the terms on which externalised memory would be organised. Gutenberg built the press. The printers who followed decided what was worth remembering — what would be printed, disseminated, and therefore preserved in the civilisation's external record. The AI analogy is precise: whoever shapes the external memory of a civilisation shapes what the civilisation can think.

***

WHAT THE LATE MOVERS FACED

The story of early adoption is incomplete without its mirror: the story of the organisations that waited. Not organisations that were ignorant or negligent, many of them were staffed by intelligent, thoughtful people who had legitimate reasons for caution. They worried about patient safety, about legal liability, about the reliability of systems that had not yet established long track records. Their caution was not irrational.

But caution has a cost that is not always visible at the time. It shows up later, when you are adapting to conditions that others have already shaped — when the protocols, the pricing norms, the patient expectations, and the regulatory frameworks have been established by the institutions that moved first. The late mover inherits a landscape it did not design. It must navigate terrain whose contours were drawn by others, often in ways that serve those others' interests and capabilities more naturally than its own.

The hospital system that waited three years before beginning to integrate predictive diagnostics did so in part because a key executive believed, sincerely, that the technology needed more validation before it was ready for clinical use. By the time he was persuaded that the validation was sufficient, the hospitals that had been running the technology for two years had accumulated something that the new adopter could not easily purchase: institutional knowledge about how to use it. Which alerts to trust and which to treat sceptically. Which patient populations generated more false positives. Which clinical contexts required more human judgment as a supplement. That knowledge — sedimented into protocols, into the habits of staff, into the informal networks of experience — was not in the user manual. It had been built through two years of use.

The late mover would eventually get there. The technology was accessible. But it would take time — more time than if the institution had been part of the early cohort — and during that time, the gap between what the experienced user could do and what the novice user could do was real, and had consequences for patients who received care from each.

This dynamic — the compound advantage of early institutional learning — is what made Gutenberg's early printing partners so powerful in the decades after the press appeared. They did not merely have access to a technology. They had developed, through practice, an understanding of how to use it that competitors who arrived later could not instantly replicate. The machine could be copied. The knowledge of how to run it efficiently, reliably, and at scale took years to develop.

There is also something more subtle happening in early adoption, something that is harder to quantify but equally important: the early mover shapes the vocabulary through which everyone else will eventually understand the technology. The terms, the frameworks, the narratives, the use cases that become standard — these are disproportionately invented by the people who arrive first, who have to make sense of something new without the benefit of existing categories. The late mover adopts not just the technology but the intellectual architecture that early movers built around it. And intellectual architecture, like physical architecture, tends to serve the needs of whoever commissioned it.

None of this means early adoption is always correct — technologies fail, early movers go bankrupt, and first-wave adopters have sometimes amplified harm alongside opportunity. Early adoption is a bet. But in a period of rapid change, the cost of caution is higher than in a period of stability. The technology does not wait. And when the late mover finally arrives, it is adopting not the technology it originally evaluated but one that has already been woven into a competitive landscape that moved around it while it waited.

***

The organisations that will matter most in twenty years are not necessarily the ones with the best technology today. They are the ones that are asking the hardest questions about what the technology is actually for, and building the capacity to use it in service of answers that are theirs.

HOSPITAL B, THREE YEARS LATER

Three years after Hospital B completed its initial integration, a researcher from a public health organisation spent two weeks interviewing physicians there about what the experience had actually been like. Not the headline metrics — diagnostic accuracy, cost per patient, system uptime — but the lived experience of navigating a significant change in how clinical judgment worked.

What she found was more complicated than the summary statistics suggested. The physicians who had embraced the integration earliest were, for the most part, satisfied with where they had arrived. They described the relationship with the system the way good clinicians describe the relationship with any reliable colleague: a source of information they trusted to be thorough and correct in specific ways, whose outputs they evaluated with their own judgment, whose occasional errors they were prepared to catch. They had not given their judgment to the system. They had developed a working relationship with it.

But a significant minority — around a third of the physicians she interviewed — described something more ambivalent. They had adapted to the system. They were performing well by the metrics the hospital tracked. But they felt, in a way they found hard to articulate, that something had changed in how they worked that they were not entirely comfortable with. One cardiologist put it this way: "I used to be very good at pattern recognition. I would see a patient and something would happen — a kind of gestalt impression — and that impression was often right. Now I'm not sure if I'm forming the impression or waiting for the system to form it and then agreeing with it. I can't tell the difference anymore."

This is not a report of failure. This physician was providing excellent care by every measurable standard. It is a report of something subtler: the permeability of the boundary between human judgment and system output when a person works closely with a capable system over a long period. The question of who is thinking what, and where the thinking is actually happening, becomes genuinely unclear.

The lesson from Hospital B is not that integration is straightforwardly good or straightforwardly problematic. It is that integration is complicated in ways that the headline metrics do not capture — and that the complications require sustained attention, ongoing conversation, and institutional humility about the limits of what performance data can tell you about what is actually happening in the minds of the people doing the work.

CHAPTER 4

Expertise Will Not Belong to Experts

"In the past, the man has been first. In the future, the system must be first."

— Frederick Winslow Taylor, The Principles of Scientific Management, 1911

Frederick Winslow Taylor was one of the most influential and most infuriating thinkers of the twentieth century, and the two qualities were related. Taylor was a mechanical engineer who, in the 1880s and 1890s, began studying factory work with the systematic precision that most people reserved for studying machines. His insight was disarmingly simple: the knowledge of how to do a job efficiently was not stored in any document or system. It lived in the minds and hands of the workers. And because it lived there — uncodified, variable across individuals, dependent on experience and judgment that could not be observed directly — it could not be optimised, standardised, or reliably transferred.

Taylor's solution was what he called "scientific management" — a systematic programme of studying work, decomposing it into its component tasks, measuring each task for efficiency, and redesigning the workflow to eliminate the variation that individual judgment introduced. The knowledge that had previously lived in the workers' minds would be extracted, analysed, and embedded in the system itself: in the tools, the layout of the factory floor, the pacing of the assembly line, the standardised procedures that every worker was trained to follow.

The consequences were enormous, and not entirely what Taylor intended. Productivity increased dramatically in the factories that adopted his methods, but the social consequences were more complicated. Workers who had previously been valued for the craft knowledge they carried found that knowledge systematically removed from the equation — their job reduced to executing steps that had been designed by someone else, at a pace that had been set by someone else, toward an outcome that had been specified by someone else. Taylor thought he was solving an efficiency problem. He was also rewriting the social contract of industrial work: the implicit agreement that a worker's knowledge and skill would be recognised and compensated as a contribution to the enterprise.

We are living through a Taylorist moment of unusual breadth and depth. Not in manufacturing; that displacement happened gradually over the twentieth century, but in knowledge work: in law, medicine, finance, consulting, engineering, design, journalism, education. The fields that the twentieth century treated as safe from automation because they required judgment and expertise are precisely the fields where the current technology is making its most visible inroads. Because what current AI systems do well — at their current level of development — is synthesise existing knowledge at scale. And synthesis of existing knowledge is a very large part of what knowledge workers do.

***

ANANYA AND MR. SHARMA

Ananya had wanted to be a lawyer since she was fourteen years old, which she recognised was a slightly unusual thing to say at a dinner party but which she had always found more clarifying than embarrassing. The clarity of the ambition had served her well: she had organised her education around it, built her networks around it, chosen her first job with a precision that impressed the partners who interviewed her and unsettled the peers who had been more improvisational about their career planning.

On her first day at the firm, a commercial law practice with a reputation built over forty years and a client base that included three of the largest corporations in the country, she had been told by the managing partner that she would spend her first two years "learning the firm's way of doing things." The phrase was used without irony. The firm had a way of doing things that had been developed over four decades, refined by the accumulated wisdom of senior partners, and transmitted to each new cohort of associates through the apprenticeship structure of legal practice. You watched how it was done. You did it under supervision. You made mistakes. You received correction. Over time, you internalized the judgment that the system encoded.

Two weeks into her first rotation, Ananya received a contract review assignment. A commercial lease agreement that had several hundred pages with clauses that a client had flagged as potentially problematic for a transaction they were considering. A standard assignment for a first-year associate: the kind of thing that would normally take three to four days of careful reading, annotation, comparison against precedents, and drafting of a risk memo.

She uploaded the document to the AI legal analysis system the firm had quietly integrated into its workflow over the preceding six months. She framed the analysis parameters carefully — the specific transaction context, the categories of risk the client was concerned about, the relevant jurisdiction's recent case law. Then she waited.

Twenty-two minutes later, she had a structured analysis. Flagged clauses with specific risk ratings. Areas where the contract deviated from market standard, with comparisons. Sections where the client's transaction context created particular exposure. Four areas marked as "requiring senior attorney review for contextual judgment" — which meant: the system identified an issue but could not fully assess how it interacted with factors that weren't in the document.

She spent two hours reviewing the analysis, checking the reasoning, identifying places where the system's interpretation of a clause seemed mechanical rather than contextually informed. She found three such places. In two of them she agreed with the system's conclusion but felt the reasoning was too narrow; in one, she believed the system had missed a relevant precedent that significantly changed the risk profile.

She printed out the analysis with her annotations and walked down the corridor to the office of Mr. Sharma, the senior partner who had been at the firm for thirty-two years and who was the acknowledged expert in commercial property law in their practice group.

He looked at what she brought him. He read it carefully — the particular attention of someone who has read thousands of documents of this type and knows exactly what he is looking for. He was quiet for a long time.

"How long did this take you?" he said.

"Twenty-two minutes to generate," Ananya said. "I've spent two hours reviewing and annotating it."

"Reviewing for what?"

"For places where the system's reasoning seems incomplete. Or where the precedent it's working from doesn't fit the specific transaction context."

He looked at her annotations. He nodded at each of them slowly, with the slight reluctance of someone confirming something they had not quite expected. "These three," he said. "These are the right ones to flag."

There was a pause. He looked at the document for another moment.

"I took six years," he said quietly, "to be able to identify the issues in this document in a first review. And to understand which ones actually matter for this type of client in this type of transaction." He was not bitter. He was accurate. "Six years of assignments like this one, building up the pattern recognition, building up the judgment about risk tolerance." He looked up at her. "What are you building?"

Ananya had thought about her answer on the walk down the corridor, because she had known the question was coming in some form. "I think I'm building the judgment layer," she said. "The part that knows when the system is right and when it's not. And the part that knows what to do with the analysis once you have it — how to use it for this client, in this context, with these stakes."

Mr. Sharma was quiet for a moment. Then he said something she did not expect: "That's a harder thing to build than what I built. Because I had thousands of hours of feedback to calibrate against, you'll have less feedback. The system will be right more often than it's wrong, which means the errors will be harder to spot and harder to learn from." He paused. "You'll need to find other ways to build the calibration."

She walked back to her office and sat with that for a while. He had not said the technology was bad or that her generation was lucky. He had said something more useful: he had identified the specific thing she would need to do differently, and had done so with the precision of someone who had spent thirty-two years thinking carefully about what legal judgment actually was.

***

WHAT SCARCITY MOVES

The staircase of expertise that Ananya had planned to climb — the orderly progression from associate to senior associate to partner, each rung earned by the accumulation of knowledge and judgment that the previous rung made possible — was not gone. It was redesigned. The bottom rungs, which had previously been about learning to do the foundational analytical work that every lawyer needed to be able to do, were now also about learning to evaluate, calibrate, and supplement the work of a system that could do much of that foundational analysis more quickly than any junior associate.

What the staircase had always been climbing toward was, in large part, the retention of knowledge, the accumulation of precedents, cases, and pattern-recognition held in a human mind and tradeable because it was rare and took years to develop. When that retention became external, the staircase did not disappear. It changed which rungs mattered. The bottom rungs, where external memory now competed most directly, became less valuable. The top rungs — judgment, context, the reading of a specific situation against accumulated wisdom — became more so.

This redesign was uncomfortable for almost everyone involved. Senior partners who had earned their expertise through a specific developmental path were not sure that the new path would produce the same quality of judgment. Junior associates who had been drawn to law in part by the promise of that developmental path were not sure what they were developing toward. Clients, who cared about outcomes rather than processes, were sometimes ahead of the profession in being willing to accept AI-assisted work that was delivered faster and more thoroughly than the traditional approach could manage.

The underlying dynamic is one that recurs in every technological displacement of expertise: scarcity does not disappear when access expands. It moves. When knowledge becomes more widely accessible, what becomes scarce is the judgment that can evaluate that knowledge — that can distinguish the correct from the plausible, the applicable from the generic, the wise from the merely informed. When analysis becomes more automated, what becomes scarce is the contextual intelligence that knows what to analyse, how to frame the question, and what to do with the answer.

Taylor's workers lost their craft expertise to the system, but they did not become unnecessary. The factories still needed people. What changed was what those people needed to do and what was valued in the *doing*. The transition was painful and was managed, in many industries, badly. The lesson was not that automation is always bad. It was that transitions are always managed by choices, and that choices made carelessly produce outcomes that choices made carefully might have avoided.

***

THE SHAPE OF WHAT REMAINS

It is worth pausing on what exactly is being displaced and what is not. The displacement of expertise is not total, even when it is substantial. What systems currently displace well is the component of expertise that is systematic: the application of known rules to available data, the synthesis of established precedents into summary assessments, the pattern-matching against large bodies of prior cases. These are real components of what professionals do: they fall within the penumbra of what can be systematized, the zone where pattern meets sufficiently abundant data. But they are not all of what professionals do.

What remains — and what, under conditions of universal access to the systematic components, becomes the locus of genuine scarcity — is the contextual layer. This is the layer that knows when the rules don't fit the situation, when the precedent is misleading because this situation is different in a way that matters, when the data is being read correctly but interpreted wrongly because the interpreter doesn't understand the specific context in which the decision must actually function. It is the layer that knows the client, the institution, the relevant personalities, the history of this particular relationship. It is the layer that understands not just what the contract says but what both parties actually want, and whether what they want is actually achievable and whether there is a better way to get it.

This contextual layer has always been present in professional work. But it was previously bundled with the systematic layer in a way that made it invisible; you hired the senior partner both for their systematic knowledge and for their contextual judgment, and it was often difficult to separate the two, because both appeared in the same billing hour from the same person. Systems are now beginning to disaggregate that bundle. The systematic component can be sourced differently. The contextual component remains scarce.

The question for every professional is whether they are investing in the component that remains scarce or the component that is becoming abundant. It is a question of what kind of professional you are trying to become — what you pay attention to, what you practice, what you value in the work that you do. The associates who arrive at depositions having read everything the system has surfaced but having formed no independent view of what it means, no hypothesis about where the case is actually weak or strong, are practicing the abundant component. The ones who use the system's output as a starting point for their own analysis — who interrogate it, refine it, situate it in the specific context of this client, this adversary, this judge — are practicing the scarce one.

Taylor understood this distinction though he articulated it from the opposite direction. He was trying to systematize the contextual knowledge of the craftsman — to capture it in protocols and measurements and procedures that could be replicated without depending on individual judgment. He largely succeeded. What he created was a world in which the systematized knowledge was abundant and relatively cheap, while the judgment that could design and oversee the system was scarce and relatively expensive. The transition that professionals are navigating now is similar in structure, inverted in direction: the systems are now doing what Taylor did to craft workers, and the judgment that will remain scarce is the kind that Taylor himself exercised — the understanding of what the system should be doing and why and when to override it.

Ananya understood this, at least partly, on the day she caught the cross-border transaction error. What she had done was not mysterious. She had read the system's output carefully, she had noticed that something in its weighting didn't match her understanding of the client's actual risk profile, she had called the client to confirm her reading, and she had adjusted the analysis accordingly. The system had been correct in its application of the general framework. She had been correct in her reading of this specific situation. Neither competence made the other redundant. Both were necessary, and they were necessary together.

***

WHAT MR. SHARMA DID

A year after his conversation with Ananya in the corridor, Mr. Sharma did something that surprised his colleagues: he restructured his practice. Not dramatically, he did not pivot to technology consulting or reinvent himself in any of the ways that the business press suggested was the appropriate response to AI disruption. He made a smaller and, in the long run, more significant change. He started spending more time with clients.

This sounds like a non-answer until you understand what had previously been crowding out that time. A significant portion of Mr. Sharma's working hours had historically gone toward the review and quality control of the analytical work produced by his junior team — the work of ensuring that the research was thorough, that the reasoning was sound, that the precedents were applicable, that the analysis held up. That work had become substantially faster to complete once the AI systems were doing more of the initial synthesis. The hours that freed up, he chose to spend on the thing that he had always believed was the real value he provided but had never quite had enough time for: understanding, in depth, what his clients actually needed.

"The best legal advice," he told a colleague at a professional development event a few years later, "is not the advice that correctly applies the law. It is the advice that correctly applies the law to what the client actually wants to achieve, which is very often not what they said they wanted when they walked in the door."

Understanding that gap between the presented question and the underlying objective had always required time and attention that the workflow had previously made scarce. The new tools had, paradoxically, made it less scarce.

This is not a universal story. Mr. Sharma is a specific person in a specific practice context, and his choices would not transfer to every professional navigating the same transition. But his story illustrates something that the headline narratives about AI and professional work consistently miss: the change is not only about what is lost. It is also about what becomes possible when the things that previously consumed time and attention are partially automated. Whether that possibility is seized depends on choices — individual and institutional — about what the freed time and attention is used for.

***

Scarcity does not disappear when access expands.

It moves.

Yesterday, scarcity looked like: who knows?

Tomorrow, scarcity will look like: who understands?

And most importantly:

Who can be trusted when the knowing comes easily to everyone?

Six months after her conversation with Mr. Sharma, Ananya had the assignment she had been quietly waiting for: a complex cross-border transaction where the AI system produced an analysis that she was not convinced was right. The transaction involved a regulatory nuance that the system had processed correctly but had weighted incorrectly given the specific risk appetite of the client. She caught it. She corrected it. And in the correction — in the specific judgment she brought to a gap that the system could not bridge — she began to understand, concretely, what she was actually building.

The risk she had caught was not hypothetical. Amazon's internal automated hiring system, shut down in 2018 after Reuters reported on its design, had been trained on ten years of the company's own hiring decisions — decisions made predominantly by human reviewers who had, over a decade, systematically favoured male applicants for technical roles. The system learned from that data and reproduced the pattern: it penalised CVs that contained the word "women's" (as in women's college, women's chess club) and downgraded graduates of all-women's colleges.

Nobody had deliberately programmed in the bias. The system had simply found it in the record of what humans had previously decided was good. What Ananya was building — the capacity to read a system's output with enough judgment to know when the system was right for the wrong reasons —

was not merely a professional skill. It was a form of institutional immune response.

PART II

The Fracture

Changing systems is one thing. Changing humans is another.

CHAPTER 5

The Contract That Quietly Expired

"The strength of the State lies in the voluntary obedience of its citizens; but the moment these cease to obey, the State dissolves."

— Jean-Jacques Rousseau, The Social Contract, 1762

In the years after the Second World War, something extraordinary happened in the industrialized world — something so ubiquitous that it became invisible, absorbed into the assumption of normality. Companies offered their employees something beyond a wage: security. You were hired with the expectation that, if you performed adequately and the company remained solvent, you would have a job. You could plan around that expectation — buy a home, raise children, think in decades rather than quarters. In exchange, you offered loyalty: you stayed, you developed expertise in the company's specific context, you subordinated a degree of your individual ambition to the collective project.

No one signed this contract. It was never articulated in a formal document. It was held in place by something more powerful than paper: mutual interest, reinforced by the post-war social and economic conditions that made long-term employment the most rational strategy for both sides. Companies that retained employees accumulated institutional knowledge. Employees who stayed accumulated seniority and the specific expertise that accumulated seniority generated. The arrangement was functional for both parties for several decades. There is an older word for this kind of mutual obligation — one that appears in ancient Indian thought but describes something universal: dharma. Not the formal rule, but the unstated duty that both parties understood and that held the arrangement together without enforcement. The social contract was, at its core, a dharmic one: each party fulfilling the role the relationship required of them. What happened when that contract broke was not just an economic disruption. It was a moral one.

Then, beginning in the 1970s and accelerating through the 1980s and 1990s, the bargain dissolved. Not with an announcement. Not with a clear moment that could be identified as the end. But gradually and then suddenly, in the way all structural changes happen: through the concatenation of individual decisions that each seemed locally rational and whose aggregate effect was a fundamental restructuring of the relationship between workers and employers. Shareholder primacy. Financialization. Globalization of labour markets. The end of the lifetime career at a single company — replaced by the portfolio career, the gig economy, the individual as their own human capital manager.

The externalisation of memory added a second layer of disruption beneath these structural shifts. The contract had been built, without anyone explicitly stating this, on the assumption that human memory retained competitive value. Expertise was worth paying for because it took years to accumulate inside a person, and that person was the only way to access it. When that accumulation became externally available — when the knowledge that had been hard-won over a decade could be approximated in seconds — the economic logic of the contract dissolved with it. The social arrangement had been built around human retention. When retention became external, the arrangement expired.

What was lost was not merely security. What was lost was the narrative structure of professional life. For most of the twentieth century, you could tell the story of your career as a progressive arc: you started somewhere, you built over time, you arrived somewhere better. The arc was not guaranteed — lives deviate from arcs, sometimes catastrophically — but it was the organising assumption, the framework within which professional choices made sense. When the long-term employment relationship eroded, the arc eroded too. What replaced it was something more contingent, more personally demanding, and considerably less legible as a life story.

***

ARJUN IN THE PARKING GARAGE

Arjun Sharma had built his career during what might, in retrospect, be called the brief Indian golden age of financial analysis: a period in the early 2000s when the combination of economic liberalization, expanding capital markets, and a shortage of experienced analysts created conditions in which a person with genuine quantitative skill and sound judgment could build a reputation quickly and trade that reputation for a career defined by its intellectual intensity. He had done exactly that. By his late thirties, he was known in his city's financial services community as someone whose calls you took and whose analysis you read.

That capacity had made him trusted. Trust, in finance, is a form of capital — more durable than money in some respects, because it takes longer to accumulate and is harder to replicate. Clients who trusted Arjun's judgment allocated time to him that they did not allocate to others. They returned his calls. They shared context that allowed him to give better analysis. The relationship compounded over time, in the way that good professional relationships do.

The shift came slowly enough that he almost missed it. It began with the data tools — systems that could pull market information, run standard analyses, and produce the kind of structured output that had previously required an analyst's time. He had seen these tools before and had not been particularly concerned. They were fast. They were not, in his judgment, wise. They could produce numbers. They could not produce the interpretation of numbers that came from understanding a specific client's context, a particular sector's dynamics, the regulatory history that shaped risk in ways that raw data did not capture.

The moment of clarity came on an ordinary Wednesday afternoon. He was presenting a strategic assessment to a client — a mid-sized manufacturing conglomerate considering a significant acquisition — when the client's CFO interrupted him midway through his analysis.

"We ran this through our system this morning," the CFO said, placing a printout on the conference table. "It gave us different numbers on the correlation between the target's margin profile and the sector's historical volatility."

Arjun looked at the numbers. He looked at his own analysis. He thought carefully. "The system's correlation is probably right for the historical data," he said. "But it's missing a regulatory change from fourteen months ago that significantly affects how you should read that volatility going forward. The change is documented but recent enough that it's underweighted in the training data."

The CFO looked at him. "How do you know that?"

"Because I was in a conference in Singapore eighteen months ago where the regulator who drafted the change explained his thinking. And I've been watching the sector closely since." He paused. "That context isn't in any dataset."

The CFO nodded slowly. He put the printout aside. But Arjun drove home that afternoon thinking about what had just happened — not the outcome, which had been fine, but the structure of the encounter. He had been required, for the first time in his career, to justify his analysis against a competing analysis that had been produced by a system. He had successfully justified it, and his justification was correct. But the CFO's question — "how do you know that?" — had a particular quality to it that Arjun could not quite name. It was not sceptical, exactly. It was more like a genuine recalibration of priors: the client was, for the first time, genuinely uncertain whether the human analyst's judgment added more than the system's analysis.

He sat in traffic for twenty minutes thinking about that uncertainty. He was not threatened by it. He understood it. He had spent his career building the kind of contextual knowledge that systems could not easily encode — the conference conversations, the relationship insights, the regulatory nuances that came from years of close attention to a specific sector. That knowledge was real. It had just been required, for the first time, to prove itself against a credible alternative.

***

WHAT ARJUN DOES NOW

The version of Arjun's work that emerged over the following two years was structured around a recognition he would have found it hard to articulate before the parking garage afternoon:

that the value he created was primarily in the layer of his judgment that could not be extracted from its context. Not the analysis, which could be produced. The reading of the analysis — the interpretation that came from knowing the specific institutional context, the regulatory environment, the relevant players and their incentives.

What changed was where he spent his time. Previously, a significant portion of his working hours had gone toward producing analysis—gathering the data, running the models, writing the reports. Those hours now went elsewhere. He spent more time in conversations with people who held context he did not yet have: regulators, industry veterans, the junior analysts who were closest to the operational realities of the sectors he covered. He spent more time thinking about framing — not just what the numbers said, but what question a client was actually trying to answer, and whether the question they had articulated was the question they actually needed to answer.

He became, in a phrase he did not invent but adopted gratefully when he heard it, an orchestrator rather than an analyst. The word captured the shift: from producing the work to directing it, interpreting it, ensuring that the system's output and the human context were brought into coherent conversation. It was work that required a different kind of attention than the analytical work had required — less systematic, more relational, more concerned with the quality of judgment than with the volume of output.

The transition was not straightforward. There were clients who, having become accustomed to the efficiency of AI-assisted analysis, now expected faster delivery across the board, including the interpretive layer, which was not. There were colleagues who had not made the transition he had made and who were delivering analysis that the systems could have produced, which created pricing pressure that was difficult to navigate. There were periods of genuine uncertainty about whether the orchestrator role he had carved out was sustainable or merely a transitional position that would eventually be automated.

What he retained, through these periods, was the conviction that the work he was doing was useful — that the clients who engaged him for the interpretive layer were getting something that they could not easily get elsewhere, and that this something was producing better decisions than the alternative. This conviction was not always sufficient to resolve the commercial pressures. But it was the foundation from which everything else was navigated.

***

RAJ, REVISITED

Around the same period, Raj — the strategy consultant who had watched his screen fill with an analysis in forty-seven seconds — came to a similar reckoning, though he arrived at it from a different direction. Raj's expertise was not sector-specific in the way Arjun's was. It was methodological: he knew how to structure strategic questions, how to run a diagnostic process, how to build consensus around a recommendation in organisations that were resistant to change. These capacities were not easily reducible to data, which had given him a degree of comfort that turned out to be partial.

What he eventually concluded — sitting with the question over several months, through conversations with clients, through watching what happened to colleagues who tried to ignore the shift — was that his value had not disappeared. It had been reorganised. The research and analysis layer of his work could now be done faster and more comprehensively by systems that he and his team should be using. The interpretive and relational layer — the capacity to understand what an analysis meant for a specific client in a specific organisational context, and to build the human coalitions necessary to act on it — remained his. What he needed to do was stop charging for the former as if it were the latter.

This was a significant professional reorientation. It required him to have difficult conversations with clients about how his work was structured and priced. It required him to retrain his team, not just technically but conceptually — to help them understand that their value was not in the hours they spent on research but in the judgment they brought to the research once it existed. Some of his team made this transition readily. Some left the firm to find positions where the old model still held. Raj watched both sets of departures with a clarity he found useful: the ones who left, in many cases, were not wrong to leave. The old model was still viable in some contexts. But those contexts were shrinking.

***

THE NARRATIVE COLLAPSE

The deepest fracture created by this disruption is not economic. It is narrative. Human beings organize their lives around stories about what their choices mean and where they are going. Professional life, for most of the twentieth century, had a recognizable story: you trained, you specialised, you built expertise over time, you were rewarded for that expertise with income, status, and a degree of security. The story was not equally available to everyone — it was easier to tell for some than for others, depending on where you started. But as a framework for making sense of your working life, it was widely shared and culturally reinforced.

That narrative is fracturing — not because expertise has become worthless, but because the relationship between expertise and its rewards is becoming less predictable, and because the specific expertise that people spent years building sometimes became substantially less valuable in a period shorter than the time they spent building it. This is the source of the particular anxiety that shows up not in unemployment statistics but in the private conversations of people who are still employed, still performing, still professionally functional — and who nonetheless feel that something has shifted beneath them that they cannot quite name.

What they are feeling is the expiration of the implicit contract. Not the economic contract — though that is changing too — but the narrative contract: the agreement, never written down but universally assumed, that sustained effort in a chosen direction would be rewarded with accumulating value. The feeling that this agreement has quietly expired, without announcement and without renegotiation, is real. It is not a feeling that is easily remedied by reassurance or by retraining programmes, because it is not primarily about skills. It is about the meaning of the investment that has already been made.

What the Gita teaches about work — that right action requires acting from duty rather than from attachment to the rewards of action — offers a frame for this moment that is not consolatory but is useful. It does not say the loss is not real. It says that the attachment to a specific form of reward, when that form is no longer available, is the source of the suffering — and that the work itself, the contribution, the application of genuine skill to genuine problems, retains its value even when the market for that value has been reorganised.

This is easier to say than to feel. But it points to something real: the expertise that Arjun, Raj, Ananya, and Maya carry does not vanish because the system can now do part of what they used to do. What vanishes is a specific economic arrangement built around that expertise. The two things — the expertise and the arrangement — are separable, even when they feel inseparable.

***

A NEW KIND OF PROMISE

Every employment relationship is, at its core, a set of mutual promises. The employee promises to show up, to apply their skills, to work toward the organisation's goals. The organisation promises to compensate that work, to develop those skills, to provide a context in which the work can have meaning. These promises have always been implicit more than explicit — subject to revision based on circumstances that neither party can fully predict.

What has changed is the rate of revision. For most of the twentieth century, the implicit promises of the employment relationship were stable enough that you could build a life around them. You could plan on a career trajectory that rewarded seniority. You could invest in a specific expertise and expect that investment to compound over a working lifetime. You could make financial and personal commitments — a mortgage, a particular city, a family structure — on the assumption that the employment arrangement that supported them would persist in something like its current form.

That stability is no longer available in the same way, and for many people it is not available at all. What the new arrangement offers instead is something different: speed, access, global reach, the ability to work with sophisticated tools that amplify individual capability in ways that were not possible before. These are real benefits. They are not consolation prizes. But they do not come with the same promise of accumulating security that characterised the old arrangement, and they require a different kind of personal adaptation than the old arrangement demanded.

The adaptation required is not primarily technical. It is existential, in the literal sense: it concerns what a working life is for, what it is organised around, what makes it meaningful. For most of the twentieth century, the answer was relatively clear: a working life was organised around the accumulation of expertise and seniority within a recognizable professional field, and it derived meaning from that accumulation and from the social role — the identity — that it conferred. The answer is becoming less clear, not because work has become meaningless, but because the container that gave it a specific shape has become less reliable.

What some people are beginning to discover — Arjun among them, Raj in his own way, Ananya with more confidence than either — is that meaning does not require the container. It requires the contribution. What made their work meaningful was not the title or the credential or the position in the hierarchy. It was the actual problem they were solving, the actual person they were helping, the actual decision they were making better than it would have been made without them. That problem, that person, that decision — these still exist. The economic arrangements around them are changing. The work itself, in the sense that matters most, has not gone away.

Arjun found this out slowly, over a period of about eighteen months. He found his way to a version of his work that was organised around judgment and context rather than analysis and synthesis — around the layer that the systems were not good at, rather than the layer they were replacing. It was less certain than the work he had done before. It required more confidence in his own reading of situations that did not have a quantitative answer. It was, he told a colleague at a conference some time later, more interesting than anything he had done in the previous decade of his career.

He said this without regret and without false consolation. The loss was real. The loss of the old arrangement — the predictability, the security, the sense of accumulating value in a form he could rely on — was real. But the loss had turned out not to be as total as he had feared in the parking garage on the afternoon when he could not explain what he did. What he could do, it turned out, was not what he had thought he was doing. The thing he could actually do — the judgment, the context, the specific knowledge of specific situations — was still needed, and in some respects needed more than before.

***

The contract did not disappear.

It changed.

And most people

are still living as though it is the same contract.

The organisations that will navigate this transition best are those that renegotiate the contract explicitly — that tell their people clearly what has changed, what remains valuable, what new skills and orientations are needed, and what the new terms of the relationship are. The ones that will navigate it worst are those that pretend nothing has changed while quietly shifting their expectations of what "performing adequately" means. That pretense is not sustainable. And it is not honest.

WHAT THE NEW CONTRACT NEEDS

The old contract had three core components: security in exchange for loyalty, development in exchange for time, and compensation that tracked accumulated expertise. The new contract, where it is being thoughtfully constructed, needs analogues of each of these — not identical versions, because the conditions that made the originals workable have changed, but genuine alternatives that provide what the originals provided.

Security in exchange for loyalty is no longer a sustainable offer for most organisations. The pace of change is too fast; the organisation's own future is too uncertain to guarantee employment security over the timescales that employees need for life planning. But security of a different kind remains possible: security in transferable skills, in professional reputation, in a network that extends beyond any single employer, in the kind of expertise that the market for talent recognises across organisational boundaries. Organizations that invest in developing these forms of portable security — that build their people's external market value, not just their internal performance metrics — are making a genuine offer, even if it is a different offer from the old one.

Development in exchange for time has become harder because the development trajectory is less clear. You can no longer promise a junior employee that, if they stay long enough, they will accumulate the same expertise as their seniors. The expertise is different now; the path to it is less well-marked. But development still matters, and organisations that take it seriously — that actively think about what their people need to learn in the next three years, that create experiences and exposure and mentorship that accelerate it — are providing something real, even if it is not the orderly staircase that the old arrangement provided.

Compensation that tracks accumulated expertise will remain important, but it will need to track a different kind of expertise accumulation than before — one organised around judgment and context rather than volume of information processed and tenure in role. The senior employee whose value is primarily in what they remember is more vulnerable than ever. The senior employee whose value is in how they think — in the quality of judgment, the depth of contextual knowledge, the maturity of the relational skills — is more valuable than ever. Compensation structures that recognise the difference between these two kinds of seniority are better aligned with the actual value being created than those that reward tenure.

None of this is a complete framework for the new social contract. The complete framework will emerge, as the old one did, from decades of negotiation, legislation, cultural development, and institutional experimentation. What is clear is that the negotiation is already underway — in the choices that organisations make about how they treat their people, in the choices that individuals make about where and how to invest their professional energy, in the choices that governments make about what workers are entitled to expect from the employment relationship. The terms of the new contract are being written right now, by all of us, whether we know it or not.

CHAPTER 6

Education After Memorization

"The aim of education is the knowledge not of facts but of values."

— William Ralph Inge, The Church and the Age, 1912

In the early nineteenth century, education in rural America happened in a single room. One teacher — often a young woman in her late teens, herself only a few years removed from being a student — presided over students ranging from six to sixteen years old, teaching reading and arithmetic and whatever else she had been able to learn before she was asked to teach. The curriculum was shaped entirely by what was available: the books in the room, the knowledge the teacher carried, the materials that could be afforded. Education was radically local, radically personal, and radically constrained by the scarcity of information.

When mass public education emerged in the late nineteenth and early twentieth centuries, reformers faced a version of the problem that every era faces when building educational systems: how do you teach a large number of people efficiently, given the resources you have? The answer they arrived at was modelled, consciously or not, on the factory: standardised curriculum, age-graded classrooms, a single teacher delivering the same content to all students at the same pace, assessment through testing that measured retention of the delivered content. The system was designed to solve the problem of information scarcity at scale. In a world where access to knowledge was limited, getting students to reliably retain the knowledge that was taught to them was important.

The design assumptions of that system have not fundamentally changed in a century and a half. We still organize education primarily around the delivery and assessment of content — around what students know, defined as what they can recall and apply in controlled conditions. The tools have updated: textbooks have been supplemented by digital resources, classrooms have gained projectors, then laptops, and now tablets. But the underlying logic — information delivered by a teacher to students who are assessed on their retention — remains the organising principle of most education in most of the world.

This logic was calibrated for a world of information scarcity. We no longer live in that world. The change that AI systems represent for education is not that they make information more accessible — the internet did that already. It is that they make the synthesis of information more accessible: the organisation, explanation, and application of knowledge that was previously available only through sustained engagement with a teacher or a curriculum. A student who in 1995 needed to ask a teacher or search a library can now ask a system that will explain, at whatever level of detail they need, in whatever format is most accessible, immediately.

***

AARAV AT MIDNIGHT

The evening Aarav's mother came to his room, it was nearly midnight. She was a secondary school teacher herself — which meant she was professionally equipped to recognise the particular quality of a teenager's late-night engagement with something that was interesting rather than merely procrastinating. The light under his door, the absence of music or other ambient sounds, the focused silence: these were the signals she had learned to read in her own students, and she read them in her son with the practiced accuracy of someone who had been doing this for seventeen years.

She knocked and opened the door. He was at his desk, three windows open on his screen, a notebook beside him with handwritten figures that he had been checking against something on the screen.

"Aarav," she said from the doorway, "it's almost midnight. You have to be up at six-thirty."

"I'm not tired, Ma."

"That's what people say when they're tired but too interested in something to stop." She came into the room and looked at the screen. "What is this?"

He tried to explain. He had been reading about the relationship between carbon capture costs and atmospheric tipping points for a class project, and the project had grown into something he could not easily stop. The reading had led to a dataset, the dataset had raised a question about the relationship between carbon pricing policy and actual corporate emissions behaviour in three different regulatory regimes, and he had been trying to model that relationship using tools the teacher had shown them but that he was now extending beyond what had been shown.

His mother was quiet for a moment. "That sounds like more than a class project," she said.

"I think it probably is," Aarav said. "But the tools are available, so I can just... look at it."

She sat on the edge of his bed. She looked at his screen — the graphs, the scenario models, the complexity of what he had built. She was not unfamiliar with the territory. She had taught geography and environmental studies for seventeen years. She knew what the questions he was asking meant and, roughly, how hard they were to answer well.

"Do you understand it?" she asked finally. "Not just the mechanics. The weight of it. What it means if the optimists are wrong about the carbon capture timeline."

Aarav was quiet for a moment. He looked at his screen. "I understand the numbers," he said. "I don't think I understand the weight yet. But I want to."

"That's honest," his mother said. She stood up. "Come to bed in half an hour. The numbers will still be there tomorrow."

She paused at the door. "The weight comes from understanding why the numbers matter," she said. "Not from looking at them longer. That's the part that takes time."

***

KAVYA AND THE CHANGED CLASSROOM

The next morning, at breakfast, Aarav asked his mother about her own work. He had been thinking about what she had said — that the weight comes from understanding why the numbers matter — and he wanted to understand how she thought about that in her classroom now, when the numbers and the context behind them were so much more accessible than they had been.

She was quiet for a moment, her tea cooling in her hands. She had been a teacher for long enough that she remembered when the scarcity of information was itself the structure of a lesson: you went to school to encounter knowledge that was not otherwise available to you, organised by someone who had spent years developing a picture you could not have assembled on your own.

"What changed," she said carefully, "is that I can't give students information they can't get elsewhere anymore. So that can't be the point. The point is what they do with the information. The question behind the question. The thing that makes one arrangement of facts more meaningful than another arrangement of the same facts."

"And is that harder to teach?" Aarav asked.

She looked at him. "It's harder to measure," she said. "Which means it's harder to be sure you're doing it right. With information delivery, you could test whether the information was retained. You could track progress. With understanding..." She paused. "You watch. You wait. You ask questions that don't have simple answers and you listen carefully to how the student navigates them."

"That sounds like it takes a long time," Aarav said.

"It does," she said. "That's the part the efficiency argument never accounts for. Understanding is not faster when the information is more accessible. It's just available to more people, which is wonderful. But building it still takes the time it takes." She looked at him with the expression he recognised as meaning she was about to say something she had been thinking about for a while. "The students who use these tools to get answers without understanding why those are the answers are going to have a very difficult time in ten years, when the systems they're in require them to evaluate answers rather than find them. That's the transition nobody's preparing them for well."

Aarav thought about his midnight modelling session. He thought about what he had been doing — not just retrieving information but building something with it, testing it against new questions, feeling the resistance of the real problem against the tools he had available. "I think I'm preparing for that," he said.

"I think you are," his mother said. "I just hope it's happening in enough classrooms that it becomes normal, rather than unusual."

***

THE QUESTION THAT SCHOOLS NEED TO ASK

What these new tools have done — and what Aarav's midnight climate modelling represents — is make proximity to complexity nearly universal. The barrier that previously separated students from sophisticated problems was not primarily intellectual. It was access: access to data, to tools, to experts, to the organised body of knowledge that would allow a sixteen-year-old to even formulate a coherent question about the relationship between carbon pricing policy and corporate emissions behaviour across regulatory regimes. That barrier has largely fallen.

This is an extraordinary opportunity. It is also a pressure: on students who now have access to complexity without necessarily having developed the capacity to navigate it well; on teachers who are required to facilitate the development of capacities that are harder to teach and harder to assess than the retention of content; on educational institutions that are structured around the delivery of information in a world where information delivery has been largely disintermediated.

The institutions that will navigate this transition well are those that can make the shift from asking "how much do you know?" to asking "how well can you think?" — and that can build the curriculum, the assessment structures, and the teacher development programmes that make this shift more than a slogan. It requires rethinking what a lesson is for, what a test is measuring, what it means to have learned something. It requires teachers who are themselves comfortable with uncertainty and capable of modelling the kind of navigation through complexity that they are asking students to develop.

These are qualities that some teachers have always had. They are not qualities that the current system reliably develops or recognises. The transition required is as much a shift in what we value in education as it is in what we teach.

***

WHAT AARAV LEARNED THAT NIGHT

Aarav's climate modelling project ran for three weeks before he presented it to his class. In the weeks of work, he made several significant errors. He misunderstood a dataset about industrial emissions and spent two days drawing conclusions from incorrectly classified data. He found a paper that appeared to support his hypothesis and used it prominently, before a conversation with his teacher revealed that the paper had been widely criticized and had not held up to replication. He built a model that produced clean, confident-looking projections without adequately accounting for the uncertainty in its underlying assumptions.

Each of these errors was identified by someone or something other than himself. The AI system flagged an inconsistency in the emissions data. His teacher pointed him to the criticisms of the paper. A peer reviewer in his class asked what would happen if the key assumptions were wrong by 20%. In each case, Aarav's first response was something like embarrassment — the feeling of having been caught out, of having been wrong in front of an audience. His second response, slower and more durable, was curiosity about how he had made the mistake and what it revealed about what he didn't yet understand.

This second response — the curiosity about the error rather than the defensiveness about it — is, educators have long recognised, the thing that actually separates learners from mere information accumulators. It is the response that turns a setback into a lesson rather than an event to be survived and moved past. It is not a response that schools, in their current form, reliably cultivate. The structures of assessment — grades, rankings, the public visibility of performance — tend to reward students who make fewer public errors, not students who learn more effectively from private ones. They tend to reward confident performance over authentic inquiry.

What Aarav was doing at midnight, with his climate model and its imperfect data, was practicing something that schools have always nominally valued and rarely actually trained: navigating genuine uncertainty in pursuit of a question that did not have a ready-made answer. He was not looking up facts. He was making choices under uncertainty, evaluating evidence of varying quality, revising his understanding when new information contradicted it, and learning to distinguish between what the data actually showed and what he wanted it to show.

These are transferable capacities. They are not subject-specific. The ability to evaluate evidence, to hold a hypothesis loosely, to understand the difference between correlation and causation, to recognise the limits of your own model — these are as useful in medicine as in climate science, as applicable in law as in engineering, as necessary in business as in academic research. They are, in fact, the capacities that Ananya was exercising when she caught the cross-border transaction error, that Maya was building when she questioned the diagnostic output, that Raj was developing when he asked what his AI system actually couldn't do.

The school that builds these capacities is not primarily teaching subjects. It is teaching a way of being in relation to knowledge — sceptical but not cynical, confident but not certain, curious about error rather than defensive about it. This is what the Socratic tradition in education has always aimed at, why the dialogue rather than the lecture was Socrates's chosen form: because genuine learning — what Plato would have recognised as anamnesis, the recollection that awakens understanding from within rather than depositing it from without — happens in the encounter with difficulty, not in the smooth transmission of established answers.

The irony is that the technology that threatens to make content transmission obsolete may also be what makes the Socratic tradition accessible for the first time at scale. A teacher with thirty students and forty minutes cannot conduct thirty simultaneous Socratic dialogues. But a student with access to sophisticated tools and a good teacher who can structure the inquiry — who can design the project, frame the question, point to the contradictory evidence, ask what happens if the assumptions are wrong — is in something closer to the old Athenian situation: one mind, in encounter with complexity, trying to understand.

***

WHAT EDUCATION IS ACTUALLY BUILDING TOWARD

There is a deeper question beneath the question of what schools should teach, and it is one that educational systems have rarely asked explicitly: what kind of person should the educated person be? Not what skills, not what knowledge — but what kind of person?

This question was central to ancient educational traditions that are largely disconnected from how we think about education today. The Platonic Academy was not teaching skills. It was forming souls — developing in students a particular orientation toward truth, toward argument, toward the examined life. The gurukul tradition in ancient India was not primarily transmitting information. It was forming character through sustained relationship with a teacher and through the practice of virtuous action alongside formal learning. The medieval university, for all its theological rigidity, was trying to produce people capable of moving from the particular to the universal — of seeing individual cases in the light of general principles and general principles in the light of particular cases.

What these traditions understood, and what modern education has largely forgotten in its focus on measurable outcomes, is that the goal of education is not to produce graduates with specific credentials but to produce people with specific qualities of mind. And qualities of mind are not produced by curriculum. They are produced by practice, by modelling, by sustained encounter with difficulty in a context that supports the development of the right response to difficulty.

The qualities that the current moment requires — the capacity to navigate genuine uncertainty, to evaluate evidence of varying quality, to act from values rather than from convenience, to hold a long-term view against short-term pressure — are exactly the qualities that education should have been building all along. The technologies that are disrupting content transmission are creating pressure to finally ask what education is actually for, and to align the practice with the answer.

It requires confronting the fact that a significant portion of what schools currently do is optimised for the wrong thing — for testable knowledge rather than for the development of judgment, for compliance rather than for the cultivation of genuine intellectual agency. The disruption is an opportunity to reckon with this, to redesign around a clearer and more ambitious goal. Whether that opportunity is seized will depend on decisions made by teachers, administrators, parents, and policymakers who are themselves embedded in institutions that resist the change they are being called to make.

The technology that makes information abundant also makes genuine inquiry — the non-abundant, the irreducibly human, the thing that only happens in the mind that has chosen to actually think — more visible, and more necessary, and in some ways more possible than it has been before. Whether schools will seize that opportunity depends on choices that have not yet been made.

***

KAVYA, ONE YEAR LATER

Kavya had been teaching secondary school for eleven years when she decided to reorganize her approach to assessment. It was not a dramatic decision — no announcement, no manifesto. She simply stopped giving tests that rewarded content recall and started giving assessments that required students to do something with what they knew.

What she was responding to, without quite having the words for it, was the externalisation of memory. Schools were built to load human minds with information that individuals would then carry throughout their professional lives. The entire structure of graded assessment — the test, the exam, the qualification — was a measure of how successfully that loading had occurred. When that information became externally available on demand, the loading became less urgent than the thing schools had always claimed was their deeper purpose but had struggled to deliver: the development of judgment that knew what to do with what memory contained.

The first year was difficult. Her students had been trained by eleven years of schooling to perform for tests, and they were good at it. When she replaced a scheduled examination with a project that required them to take a position on a contested policy question, using evidence they had to evaluate themselves, a significant portion of the class was confused about what she wanted. They had learned to find the right answer. She was asking them to construct one.

One student — a quiet, methodical girl named Priya who had always scored highly on conventional assessments — came to see her after the first project was returned. "I don't understand what I did wrong," she said. "I used all the sources you gave us. I organised them properly. I cited everything."

"You did all of that correctly," Kavya said. "What I'm asking is different. I want to know what you think is true about this question. Not what the sources say. What you think is true, based on the sources, and why."

Priya was quiet for a moment. "But what if I'm wrong?"

"Then we learn from why you were wrong," Kavya said. "That's also learning."

Priya looked like she was being asked to do something physically uncomfortable. And she was — she was being asked to make herself vulnerable in a way that the previous eleven years had taught her to avoid. Performing correctly was safe. Thinking visibly was not, because thinking visibly meant being wrong in ways that couldn't be hidden.

The culture shift that Kavya was trying to produce in her classroom — from performance to inquiry, from correctness to thinking — is the same culture shift that every institution navigating this transition needs to produce at a larger scale. It requires tolerating the discomfort of visible uncertainty. It requires redesigning reward structures so that genuine engagement is recognised alongside correct answers. It requires teachers and administrators who are themselves willing to demonstrate the kind of learning-from-error that they are asking students to practice.

Two years later, Priya was one of the strongest students in Kavya's class. Not because she had become less rigorous — her research was still thorough, her citations still careful. But she had learned to bring a perspective to the material rather than just organising it. She had learned to ask what she thought, and to be willing to be wrong about it in the presence of someone who would help her understand why.

Kavya's instinct — that the goal was not to prevent students from using AI but to ensure they used it in ways that built rather than displaced genuine understanding — had a counterpart in the Khan Academy's early experiments with an AI tutoring assistant called Khanmigo, launched in 2023. Unlike tools designed to give correct answers, Khanmigo was explicitly programmed to never directly answer a student's question. It would instead ask a question back: what do you think is the first step? What have you tried? Where does this approach break down? Early assessments suggested that students who used Khanmigo showed different learning trajectories than those using answer-giving AI tools — not faster, but deeper, with better retention and more demonstrable understanding. The tool had been designed around a theory of learning rather than a theory of efficiency. The distinction was exactly what Kavya had been trying to articulate to her department for three years. It had taken a product, not a pedagogical argument, to make it visible.

***

The question that schools built for information scarcity asked:

How much can you remember?

The question that genuine education asks

has always been something harder:

How deeply can you understand?

That question has not changed.

Only the urgency of asking it.

CHAPTER 7

When Work Stops Defining Worth

"Blessed is he who has found his work; let him ask no other blessedness."

— Thomas Carlyle, Past and Present, 1843

On January 5, 1914, Henry Ford announced that the Ford Motor Company would henceforth pay its workers five dollars a day — roughly double the prevailing wage in American manufacturing. The announcement caused an immediate sensation. Ford plants were besieged by job applicants, some of whom had travelled hundreds of miles on the strength of the rumor. Newspapers treated the announcement as a social event of the first order. Editorialists debated whether Ford was a visionary or a fool. Competing manufacturers calculated whether they could survive the wage competition.

Ford's public rationale was that he wanted his workers to be able to afford the cars they were building — a statement that contained a genuine insight about the relationship between production and consumption that would become a cornerstone of twentieth-century economic thinking. But the private rationale was more immediate: Ford's plants were experiencing ruinous turnover. Workers left after short periods because the work was brutal — the assembly line moved at a pace designed to maximise output, and the physical and psychological demands of keeping up with it drove people to quit in numbers that made continuity of production difficult. The five-dollar day was, in part, a retention mechanism.

What Ford did not fully anticipate was the cultural consequence of what he had built. By creating a wage that allowed his workers to participate in consumer society — to buy houses, to save, to plan futures — he had done something more significant than improve their material circumstances. He had given work a social meaning it had not previously had at that scale. Industrial labour became, for the first time, the basis of a middle-class life. The factory worker who had previously been understood as a proletarian — a person defined by their lack of property and their dependence on wage labour — became, over the following decades, a citizen: someone with a stake in the economic and political order, with interests worth taking seriously.

The deeper consequence of Ford's decision was not economic but cultural. By paying workers enough to participate in the consumer economy, Ford had inadvertently created the conditions for work to become the central organising institution of personal identity in the twentieth century. What you did for a living became, to an unprecedented degree, who you were. Your job determined not only your income but your social networks, your daily rhythms, your sense of competence and purpose, your place in the community. This arrangement was not inevitable. It was constructed by the particular economic and social conditions of the mid-twentieth century, reinforced by the institutions and cultural norms that those conditions produced.

***

RAHUL AND THE TUESDAY IN OCTOBER

Rahul had worked at the same technology company for eleven years. He knew the building the way you know a place you have spent a significant portion of your adult life in: the way the light changed in the open-plan area at different times of day, the particular sound the elevator made on the third floor, the coffee machine on the fourth floor that had been broken for a year and a half and that nobody had replaced because there was a perfectly functioning machine on the fifth floor. The escalation of a work order felt disproportionate.

The announcement came on a Tuesday in October, delivered by the VP of Operations in a presentation that had clearly been prepared with the assistance of a communications consultant. The language was specific in its vagueness: the company was "restructuring to position itself for a more automated future," which meant, as everyone in the room understood within the first three minutes, that the data analysis and reporting functions were being largely automated and that the team of thirty people who had been performing those functions was being reduced to eight.

Rahul heard the number and did the arithmetic immediately, the way you do when numbers have personal stakes. Thirty to eight. Twenty-two people. He had worked with most of them for years. He was fairly confident — ninety percent confident, which is the limit of confidence available to anyone in that situation — that he was one of the eight. He was not sure whether that made it better or worse.

Priya, who sat two rows ahead of him, received the announcement without visible reaction. Priya was one of the best analysts on the team, possibly the best, and had been at the company for eight years. She had joined after completing a postgraduate degree in data science. She had turned down three external offers in the previous two years because she was comfortable where she was and did not feel the urgency of the job market pulling at her. She had believed, as most people in their position believe, that doing good work was the primary protection against the kind of risk that was now, on a Tuesday in October, sitting in the room with her.

The goodbye drinks were held the following Friday at the bar near the office that the team had used for years. The gathering had the particular atmosphere of professional events that carry grief they cannot quite name: everyone was performing a degree of good cheer that was genuinely felt in patches and genuinely performed in others, and the mixture of the two was harder to navigate than pure grief would have been. People talked about plans. They exchanged information about job markets, mutual contacts, reference letters. They drank more than they normally would on a Friday.

At some point in the evening, Rahul found himself standing with Priya at the bar, both of them looking at the room rather than at each other.

"Are you okay?" he asked.

"I don't know yet," she said. "Ask me in six months." She took a sip of her drink. "I keep thinking I should be angrier than I am. But I'm mostly just confused."

"About what?"

"About what I was actually doing there," she said. "Eleven years. I thought I understood what the work was. And then I watched that presentation, and I realised I'd been doing something that could be automated, and I had never quite seen it that way because nobody ever said it that way. Nobody said: what you're doing is pattern recognition applied to data. They said: you're an analyst. You're part of the team. You're good at this." She paused. "Nobody lied. But nobody said the full truth either."

***

THE FULL TRUTH

Nobody lied. That is what makes the current disruption different from previous ones in ways that matter for how we respond. Previous rounds of automation — the mechanization of agriculture, the automation of manufacturing — displaced workers from specific tasks through direct substitution. The machine did the task instead of the person. The relationship between the person and the task was at least clearly visible. What is happening now is subtler: the work continues to exist, in a form that looks similar from the outside, but the human contribution to it has been reorganised in ways that were not communicated and are not always obvious until the reorganisation has already happened.

When Priya said "nobody lied," she was describing something important. Her employer had not deceived her about the nature of her role. It had simply not examined it in a way that would have revealed its vulnerability. The people who managed her had been operating within the same assumption she had been operating within: that the skills she had accumulated — her ability to identify patterns in data, to produce structured reports, to contextualize findings for specific business units — were stable assets, valuable in the way that specialised skills are valuable.

What changed was not Priya's skill or the quality of her work. What changed was the market for that skill, when it became clear that systems could produce its outputs more quickly and at a fraction of the cost. The expertise that Priya had spent eight years developing had been, in some important sense, the wrong expertise to develop — not wrong in absolute terms, but miscalibrated for the world that was arriving as she was developing it. And nobody had told her, because nobody around her had seen it coming clearly enough to say so.

What had been miscalibrated was not Priya's intelligence or her commitment. It was the assumption that the value of her expertise lay in what she had accumulated inside herself — the patterns she had learned to recognise, the context she had built up over years, the data relationships she could see without being told to look. That accumulation had been valuable because it was difficult to replicate. When it became externally replicable, the value of holding it inside shifted. What she had built was, in the deepest sense, external memory before external memory existed as a concept. The systems simply did it faster.

This is also where the concept introduced in the Preface of this book — dharma, the Sanskrit idea of acting according to what one's role and nature actually require — offers something surprisingly practical to a twenty-first-century technology story. The Gita's teaching on work is that one should act without attachment to the fruits of action: from duty and genuine contribution rather than from the desire for specific rewards. This is sometimes misread as passive or fatalistic. It is in fact the opposite. It is a teaching about where to anchor your sense of worth when external rewards become unreliable. Priya's crisis was, at bottom, a dharmic one: she had anchored her identity in the specific reward — the analyst role, the salary, the daily structure — rather than in the underlying contribution that the role had been delivering. When the reward changed, the identity collapsed, because the anchor had been in the wrong place. The worker who has anchored their identity in the genuine application of skill to genuine problems — in the actual contribution rather than the credential — is less devastated by the reorganisation of the market for that work than the worker who has anchored it in the specific form the reward had previously taken. This is not comfortable to say to someone who has just lost their job. It is still true.

***

WHAT REPLACES IDENTITY

The question that Priya could not quite answer at the bar — what she had actually been doing — is the question that a significant portion of the professional workforce is wrestling with in one form or another. Not "what is my job title?" but "what is the actual contribution I am making, and what is its value, and to whom?" These questions were always worth asking. They become urgent when the economic arrangements that had previously made the asking unnecessary — that had provided a stable answer through the structure of employment — are no longer stable.

The answers to those questions, when people find them, tend to look different from what they expected. The contribution that survives automation is rarely the most visible, most easily described part of the job. It is the relational and contextual and judgment-dependent layer: knowing the specific person's concerns, understanding the institutional history, recognising when a technically correct answer is contextually wrong, maintaining the trust that allows difficult recommendations to be heard. These contributions are real. They are valuable. They are not easily captured in job descriptions and are not easily replaced by systems.

But they require a different relationship with work than the one that most professional culture has built. They require the ability to define your contribution in terms of outcomes and relationships rather than in terms of tasks and credentials. They require the capacity to be useful in ways that are not immediately legible as a job — not "I am a data analyst" but "I am someone who understands the specific context of this organisation's decisions and can apply that understanding to whatever analytical resources are available."

That shift — from identity-as-credential to identity-as-contribution — is the psychological transition that the current moment requires. It is difficult. It is made more difficult by institutions that continue to organize themselves around credential-based hierarchies and task-based job descriptions, providing insufficient support for people attempting to make the shift. But it is the shift that the moment requires, and the people who make it — who find ways to define their value in terms that do not depend on the specific tasks that systems are now performing — will be better positioned to contribute meaningfully in the world that is arriving.

***

THE PEOPLE WHO NAVIGATE IT WELL

The people who navigate the transition from identity-as-credential to identity-as-contribution tend to share certain characteristics. They are not necessarily the most technically sophisticated. They are not always the most credentialed. They are, characteristically, people who have maintained some part of their selfhood outside the job — who have held onto interests, relationships, capacities, and curiosities that were not entirely consumed by the professional identity that employment provided.

This sounds like a therapy prescription — be a whole person, have hobbies — and in one sense it is. But the observation is not primarily psychological. It is structural. The people who have invested entirely in their professional identity, who have allowed the job to provide all of the structure, social connection, meaning, and self-regard that they previously organised their life around, are the ones who find the transition hardest. Not because they are weaker or less resilient. Because the thing they are losing is everything — and that total investment is not a personal failing but an atavistic response to the industrial-era bargain: the world told them the job was the container of their worth, and they believed it, as generations before them had believed it too.

For Rahul, the hardest part was not the financial uncertainty, though that was real. It was the disruption of a daily structure that had organised his life for eleven years. He woke up at the same time. He took the same route to the office. He had the same conversations with the same people in the same building, variations on the same professional themes, and those conversations and their repetition were not empty: they were the texture of a life, the substance of a decade of professional relationship that were genuinely his and genuinely mattered to him. When that structure disappeared, it left not just a financial gap but a structural one — no reason to be somewhere at a particular time, no external demand around which to organize the day, no community of people who expected him and whom he expected in return.

His recovery — which is what it was, though he would not have called it that — happened partly through the deliberate reconstruction of structure. He joined a volunteer organisation connected to his former industry, partly for the networking and partly because he needed somewhere to go on Tuesday mornings. He started working on a technical certification that he had been intending to pursue for years and had never found time for. He began having lunch with people outside his former workplace — an expansion of network that felt awkward at first and gradually produced the professional relationships that eventually led to his next position.

None of this was graceful. Rahul would be the first to say so. There were months that were difficult, when the uncertainty was not a backdrop but the foreground — when the primary experience of each day was not "doing something" but "waiting to find out what would happen." That waiting is the hardest part of any transition, and no amount of advice about resilience or growth mindset makes it comfortable. The waiting is simply the cost of the transition, and it is borne differently by different people depending on their financial cushion, their family support, their professional network, and their capacity to tolerate uncertainty — none of which are distributed equally.

What Rahul found, on the other side of the waiting, was a version of professional life that was smaller in some ways and larger in others. Smaller in the sense of institutional scale — he was no longer part of a large organisation with the resources and reach that implied. Larger in the sense of scope: his new role required him to draw on a wider range of his capabilities than his previous one had, because the organisation he joined was too small to maintain the specialised divisions that his former employer had staffed. He wore more hats. He made more decisions without the organisational context that had previously made the decisions for him. He understood, more directly than before, the connection between what he did and what happened as a result.

He was, in some ways, doing more of what work actually is — the application of judgment to problems, the translation of capability into contribution — with less of the organisational scaffolding that had previously mediated the connection. It was, in the end, not the outcome he would have chosen in the parking lot the night of the goodbye drinks. But it was not the catastrophe he had feared either.

***

WHAT WORK CANNOT PROVIDE ANYMORE

There is a function that employment has provided, for roughly a century of industrial-era professional life, that has nothing to do with income and nothing to do with skill development. It is the provision of community — not the deep community of family and chosen friendship, but the intermediate community of regular collective activity, the people you see predictably, the shared project that gives you common reference, the social rituals — the lunch table, the after-work drink, the hallway conversation — that fill the middle distance of a working life.

This intermediate community is not trivial. Robert Putnam, in his research on social capital, distinguished between "bonding capital" — the deep ties of close relationships — and "bridging capital" — the weaker but broader ties of acquaintance and professional association that connect individuals to wider social networks and opportunities. Employment, for most people, was one of the primary sources of bridging capital. The colleague you did not know well but saw daily. The professional contact who knew someone who might be useful. The sense of being part of something — an organisation, an industry, a profession — that extended beyond your immediate personal circle.

When employment structures become less stable, this bridging capital is disrupted along with the income and the professional identity. The person who loses a long-term position does not merely lose a paycheck. They lose a community, however attenuated. They lose the predictable human contact that organised their week. They lose the professional networks that were maintained through regular presence in a shared environment. These losses are real and are not adequately captured in unemployment statistics.

They are also, in an era when AI systems are increasingly handling the transactional layer of professional work, becoming more widespread — not just among those who lose positions, but among those who stay in them. The work that sustained the intermediate community was partly the work itself — the collaboration, the joint problem-solving, the meetings that felt redundant in the moment and turned out to be how people built understanding of each other. As more of that work shifts to automated systems, and as remote work further attenuates physical community, the intermediate social structure that employment provided is eroding.

What replaces it is not obvious. Some people find it in professional communities organised around identity rather than employer — industry associations, alumni networks, practitioner communities — that provide the bridging capital that a single employer once provided more reliably. Some find it in deliberately constructed social contexts: the regular dinner, the sports team, the volunteer organisation, the neighbourhood project. These require more intentional effort than the community that employment provided automatically, but they are available, and for people who invest in them, they work.

The communities that survive and thrive through this transition will be those that can build these intentional intermediate communities — that can give people a place to belong that is not entirely dependent on a single employer's continuity. This is partly an individual challenge and partly an institutional one. It requires organisations to think seriously about what kind of community they provide and how to preserve it through transitions that would previously have been purely economic events.

***

WHAT MEANING ACTUALLY REQUIRES

The question of meaning in work is ancient, but its contemporary form is new. Previous generations faced it primarily as individuals — why am I doing this, does it matter, is there more to life than this particular role? The question was personal and philosophical, and while it could be acute, it was usually navigated within a social structure that did not itself seem threatened. The institution remained. Your place within it might be dissatisfying, but the institution offered continuity that individual dissatisfaction could not undermine.

What is new is that the question is now structural. Not: is my work meaningful? But: what is work's relationship to meaning when the cognitive functions that once made work distinctively human — the analysis, the synthesis, the pattern recognition, the translation of information into decisions — are being performed by systems at a fraction of the cost and a multiple of the speed? If those functions are no longer distinctively human, what is?

Ancient philosophy does not fully anticipate this question — but it is far from useless for it. The Bhagavad Gita's central insight — that one should perform the work appropriate to one's nature and station without attachment to its fruits — has something relevant to say here. The attachment to outcomes is the source of the anxiety. Arjuna was paralysed not by the difficulty of the task but by his attachment to specific results: the preservation of people he loved, the particular shape of the world that he wanted to emerge from the battle. When Krishna released him from that attachment, the task became possible.

The parallel for our moment is this: the anxiety around AI and work is largely an anxiety about outcomes — about income, status, identity, the specific forms of contribution that have been the basis of professional self-regard. When we hold those outcomes loosely enough to ask what the work is actually for — what human capability is actually serving, what genuine need is being met — the question becomes less existential and more practical. And practical questions have practical answers.

What AI systems cannot provide is presence. Not physical presence — that is a simpler matter — but the kind of presence that a physician brings to a patient who is frightened, that a teacher brings to a student who is confused, that a counselor brings to a person in crisis, that a colleague brings to someone navigating a difficult professional situation. The presence of a human being who is actually attending — who has skin in the outcome, who brings to the encounter not just information and analysis but care, judgment, and the full weight of a human life's worth of understanding what it is to be in the situation the other person is in. These are not small things. They are not automatable. They are, in fact, increasingly scarce in a world where the transactional layer of human interaction is being steadily absorbed by systems that are cheaper and faster.

Rahul, in his new position, was doing more of this kind of work than he had done before. Not because his previous employer had been indifferent to human connection — it had not been — but because the organisational structure of a large institution creates distance. Things go through channels. Relationships are mediated by process. The human element is present but filtered. At a smaller organisation, working directly with colleagues on problems where the outcome mattered to everyone in the room, Rahul was closer to the actual purpose of the work than he had been in eleven years of organisational mediation. He had lost the institutional identity. He had found something that, slowly and imperfectly, was taking its place.

This is not a story with a clean moral. Not everyone who loses institutional employment finds a better configuration on the other side. The transition is costly, unequal in its distribution of costs, and dependent on factors — financial cushion, family support, professional network, health, temperament — that have nothing to do with the quality of the person going through it.

The story of individual navigation through structural transition is not a substitute for the structural response that the transition requires. Both are needed.

But the individual dimension of the story matters too, because the structural response — whatever form it takes — will not insulate people entirely from the experience of having to navigate changed circumstances. The skills that help people navigate are real skills. They can be taught, cultivated, and supported. They are not equally distributed now, but they do not have to remain as unequally distributed as they currently are. Part of what this transition requires — in education, in professional development, in how we think about work's relationship to identity — is building those skills more broadly, so that the structural disruption, when it comes, is encountered by people who have the internal resources to navigate it rather than people who have been given every expectation of stability and nothing to draw on when the stability ends.

***

Rahul found Priya six months later, at an industry event. She had started consulting — working with three companies on the kind of data analysis projects that she was now delivering more quickly, using tools she had been using when she worked for her employer. The market for her actual skill, the contextual judgment, the business translation, the knowing-which-numbers-matter was larger than she had realised. What she had lost was the employment wrapper that had made the skill invisible. What she had found, with some difficulty, was the skill itself.

Their story had a cautionary counterpart in a widely cited case from Sweden. In 2023, Klarna's CEO announced that the company's AI customer service assistant was handling the work of approximately 700 full-time agents, managing two-thirds of all customer chats. The announcement was treated as a landmark moment in the automation of service work. The AI system handled volume effectively. What it struggled with were the edge cases — the escalated complaints, the emotionally complex interactions, the situations that required judgment about when a policy should be applied differently from how it was written. The efficiency metrics had not captured that dimension of the work. What the metrics had measured — speed, throughput, resolution rates on standard queries — turned out to be a partial picture of what customer service actually required. The announcement had described how much the system could do. It had been quieter about what it could not. What had looked like an end point had been a first chapter. The work itself had not disappeared. The understanding of what the work actually required had not been fully accounted for in the initial claim.

CHAPTER 8

Democracy Under Cognitive Pressure

"If a nation expects to be ignorant and free, in a state of civilisation, it expects what never was and never will be."

— Thomas Jefferson, Letter to Charles Yancey, January 6, 1816

The committee room in the ministry building smelled of recycled air and tepid coffee. Sara Nair had sat in this room hundreds of times — first as a parliamentary researcher in her mid-twenties, then as a policy advisor, then as the person who briefed the people who briefed the ministers. She knew which chairs creaked. She knew which fluorescent light flickered every forty seconds above the third seat on the left. She knew which corner of the room had a dead mobile signal. She knew the room the way you know a place you have spent too much of your life inside.

But on this particular Tuesday morning, watching the minister struggle to answer a question about AI-generated political content, Sara felt she was in a room she had never visited before.

The question had come from a backbencher on the opposition side — a young MP named Arjun Mehta who had won his constituency just eighteen months earlier and still had the unsettling habit of asking exactly the questions that nobody wanted to answer. He stood, adjusted his glasses, and asked, in a voice that was almost apologetic in its precision: "Minister, can you tell us how many of the 340,000 social media posts currently circulating about the government's infrastructure bill were generated by automated systems rather than written by human citizens?"

The minister paused. He was a capable man — Sara had worked with him for four years, had written three major policy papers under his guidance, and genuinely respected his judgment. But the pause told her everything. Because the answer was: nobody knew. And more troublingly, nobody had thought to measure it before it became a crisis.

"We are examining that data," the minister said finally.

"With respect, Minister," the young MP replied, his voice still quiet, "the bill comes to a vote in eleven days."

Sara looked down at the briefing on her tablet. She had spent three weeks refining it, running it through independent models, checking it against forty-seven stakeholder consultations. It was thorough. It was evidence-based. And sitting in that room, she understood with a clarity that felt like cold water that her briefing was almost certainly not the document that would decide the vote. Economic projections would not decide the vote. It would be decided by what those 340,000 posts — human or automated — had already planted in the minds of legislators who read social media on their phones during recesses, in cabs, during the long hours of parliamentary session when the debate had grown stale.

She typed to her assistant: "Find out if we have any analysis on those posts. Content origin, timing, velocity, network structure. Anything." The reply came back in four minutes: "Nothing systematic. We can start now. Eleven days may not be enough."

Sara set down her tablet and watched the minister navigate a question that the architecture of modern democracy had never been designed to handle.

***

LUTHER'S NINETY-FIVE THESES

On the morning of October 31st, 1517, a theology professor named Martin Luther wrote out ninety-five propositions he wished to debate — careful academic arguments about church practice, specifically the sale of indulgences. According to tradition, he nailed them to the door of the Castle Church in Wittenberg. This was a standard academic invitation. Faculty members posted notices on church doors all the time. The door was essentially a public bulletin board.

What Luther did not account for was the technology that Johannes Gutenberg had unleashed sixty years earlier.

Within two weeks of Luther's posting, printed copies of his Ninety-Five Theses were circulating across Germany. Within two months, they had reached England, France, Italy, and Spain. Within a year, they had been translated into German, French, Dutch, and English and were being discussed in university halls and market squares across a continent. The church, which commanded fifteen centuries of institutional authority and a communication infrastructure built on cathedral hierarchies and papal encyclicals, could not respond fast enough. By the time Rome had formulated its official reply, Luther's arguments had already taken root in places Rome could not easily reach.

The church's response was not wrong, exactly. It was slow. The theological arguments it marshaled against Luther were reasonable. The institutional authority it invoked was real. What the church could not match was the pace of propagation that the printing press enabled. A handwritten reply travelled at the speed of a messenger. Luther's printed theses travelled at the speed of commerce — moving through the same networks that moved wool and spices and books, at a velocity that papal bureaucracy could not approach.

The printing press did not create the Protestant Reformation. The ideas behind it had circulated for centuries. Jan Hus had argued similar things a hundred years before Luther. Hus was burned at the stake in 1415. His movement faded. Luther was not burned. He survived. And the decisive difference was not the quality of his arguments. It was the speed at which those arguments travelled — and the fact that, once printed and distributed, they could not be recalled.

This is the pattern that repeats whenever communication technology accelerates beyond the capacity of institutions to respond: the systems designed for slow information encounter fast information, and they begin to fracture. Not dramatically. Gradually, and then suddenly — and by the time the fracture is visible, the damage is already structural.

What we are experiencing now operates at a categorically different speed. Systems can generate a hundred thousand persuasive, personalised, emotionally calibrated messages in the time it takes a human to write one. The speed differential is not incremental — it is categorical. And the institutions designed for measured deliberation are facing it without adequate preparation or historical precedent.

***

WHAT THE YOUNG ALREADY KNOW

There is an asymmetry in how this disruption is being experienced across generations that is worth naming explicitly, because it has implications for how the response needs to be organised.

People who grew up with social media — who have spent their formative years in information environments governed by algorithmic amplification — have a different and in some ways more accurate intuitive model of how information spreads than people who formed their information habits before those environments existed. They know, from the inside, that content travels for reasons that have little to do with its accuracy. They have seen things go viral that were demonstrably false and things that were demonstrably true sit ignored. They have watched communities cohere around shared fictions. They have participated, often unknowingly, in the mechanics of amplification — sharing things that turned out to be wrong, contributing to the spread of narratives they later wished they had not.

This is not a comfortable knowledge to have. But it is a more accurate model of the information environment than the model that many institutions — media organisations, political parties, educational systems, governments — continue to operate from. Many institutional responses to the disinformation challenge are still organised around the premise that if accurate information is made available, people will choose it. This is not how information environments governed by engagement algorithms work. Accuracy and visibility are independent variables. The institutional response that treats them as correlated is solving the wrong problem.

The young people who have grown up inside these environments understand this, often without being able to articulate it. They have developed, through experience, a scepticism that is sometimes healthy and sometimes tips into cynicism — an inability to trust any source because the environment has made source verification difficult. The healthy version of this scepticism is an asset. The cynical version is a problem: a population that cannot distinguish reliable information from unreliable is not a population capable of democratic self-governance.

What the young understand that older generations often do not is that the response to manipulated information environments is not, primarily, more information. It is structural: it requires changing the incentive structures that produce the manipulation, building the institutional infrastructure to authenticate and contextualize, developing the civic habits that allow people to evaluate what they encounter. Sara understood this. Her legislation was an attempt at one part of the structural response. She also understood that it was one part of a response that needed to be much larger.

***

SARA'S CRISIS

Sara had not gone into public policy because she believed government was efficient. She had gone in at twenty-four because she believed — with the particular stubbornness of someone who had read enough history to know how badly things go wrong when institutions fail — that functioning democratic systems were the only reliable protection against the concentrated power of the few. She had spent fifteen years holding that belief the way some people hold religious faith: not without doubts, but as a foundational premise that the rest of her work depended on.

The first serious crack appeared on a Monday evening in the middle of winter. She was at her desk at eleven o'clock, working on a climate adaptation brief, when her phone lit up with a news alert: a major piece of social infrastructure legislation her team had been supporting — eighteen months of research, consultations with forty-seven stakeholder groups, three rounds of public comment — had become the subject of a coordinated online controversy that had erupted in the previous six hours.

By midnight, the controversy had accumulated hundreds of thousands of impressions. By two in the morning, three opposition MPs had issued public statements calling for a review. By the time Sara arrived at work the following morning, the minister was being questioned about it at a doorstep press conference.

She pulled up the overnight analysis. The viral content made claims that were, to anyone who had spent eighteen months working on the policy, demonstrably incorrect — not misleading but factually wrong in specific, verifiable ways. The legislation said the exact opposite of what the posts claimed. The text was publicly available. Anyone could check.

But "anyone could check" turned out to be a phrase that described almost nobody. Because the posts did not require the legislation to say what they claimed it said. They only required enough people to feel uncertain about what it actually said — to hold a residue of doubt. Confusion was the product.

And the product was travelling at a velocity that democratic deliberation had never been designed to match.

She called the minister at seven in the morning.

"How bad is it?" he asked.

"The content is factually wrong," she said. "Demonstrably, checkably, textually wrong. But it has 2.3 million impressions and counting."

A silence.

"And our correction?" he said.

"Forty-seven thousand," Sara said. "As of six minutes ago."

Another silence. Then: "So we're losing by a factor of fifty."

"Yes. And the gap is widening."

The minister let out a long breath. "What do we do?"

Sara had been awake most of the night thinking about exactly this question. She had no good answer. The tools available to a democratic government for responding to fast-moving misinformation were all tools designed for a different era. Press conferences, official statements, formal corrections, media briefings. They moved at the speed of deliberation: measured, careful, attributed, accountable. The content they were trying to respond to moved at the speed of algorithmic amplification: instantaneous, frictionless, optimised for emotional resonance.

"We respond the way we always respond," Sara said. "Clearly, accurately, on the record. And we accept that in the short term, it may not be enough."

"And the vote?"

"I don't know," Sara said. It was the first time in fifteen years of public service that she had said those words to a minister and genuinely meant them.

There was a longer silence after that. She could hear him breathing. In fifteen years she had given ministers options they did not want, projections that delivered bad news, legal opinions that constrained preferred courses of action. She had never delivered a silence of this quality — the particular silence of an honest expert who could not offer a clear path.

"What if we commission an independent review?" the minister finally asked. "An external body — academics, technical people — to assess the content and issue a formal correction?"

"We can do that," Sara said. "It will take four to six weeks minimum. The post will have reached thirty million impressions by then. The review's findings will reach perhaps three hundred thousand."

"Media briefings?"

"We've already briefed six journalists. Four have written corrections. Two have written additional stories using the misinformation as a hook because it was generating more traffic. The corrections have fewer than a tenth the reach of the original content."

The minister was quiet again. Then he said something Sara had not expected. "Tell me something, Sara. When did we build the system that makes this possible? When did we agree to this?"

She thought about it. The real answer was that they had not agreed to it. No democratic body had ever debated a proposition reading: "Resolved, that private companies shall have the right to distribute content in algorithmically optimised ways, with priority given to content that maximises engagement regardless of accuracy." No parliament had voted on that. No public consultation had explored those trade-offs. The architecture had assembled itself incrementally — each individual step small, each business decision rational from within its own frame — until the aggregate structure was something nobody had designed but everyone had built.

"We didn't build it," Sara said. "It assembled itself while we were doing other things."

"Is there a difference?"

"Legally, yes. Morally, I'm less certain."

Another silence. Then: "What do we actually need? Not for this bill. For the long problem."

Sara had not been asked this question by a minister before. They usually asked about the immediate political management of a crisis — what to say, to whom, in what sequence. The long problem was something she had been thinking about in her spare time, in the margins of her actual work, because it felt too large and too slow for the pace at which policy operated.

She answered anyway. She told him about the information literacy gap — the generational asymmetry between the people who built the current information environment and the citizens expected to navigate it. She told him about provenance infrastructure: the emerging technical capacity to watermark and attribute synthetic content, which existed but had no regulatory mandate and no institutional backbone. She told him about the deliberation gap — that democratic institutions were optimised for a world in which information travelled slowly enough to be evaluated before it was acted upon, and that this was no longer the world they were governing.

She told him all of this in about four minutes, because she had been thinking about it for months and the words came quickly. When she finished, the minister said nothing for a moment.

"That's not a communications problem," he said finally. "That's an infrastructure problem."

"Yes," Sara said.

"And we've been treating it like a communications problem."

"That's what we have tools for."

She heard him exhale. "We'll schedule the briefing. We'll do the formal correction. We'll brief the chair of the select committee. We'll do everything we can with the tools we have." A pause. "And you'll write me a memo on the long problem. Properly. Give me something I can take to cabinet."

"Yes," Sara said.

She hung up the phone and sat in the quiet of her office, the gray morning light coming through the window, the city beginning to wake outside. She had a bill to manage. She had a minister to brief. She had a crisis communications schedule to run.

She also had a memo to write about a problem that was larger than any single crisis, any single minister, any single democratic system's capacity to address alone. And she understood, with a clarity she had not had at midnight when she first saw the impressions numbers, that the memo was probably the more important task.

***

THE ARCHITECTURE OF SLOW THINKING

Democracy was not designed for speed. This is not a flaw — it is the point. Democratic institutions are deliberately slow because the decisions they make matter too much to be made quickly. Laws, rights, resource allocations — these require deliberation precisely because the consequences of getting them wrong are severe and often irreversible. The friction is the protection.

James Madison understood this. The American constitutional framers built deliberate friction into their system — checks and balances, bicameral legislatures, judicial review — specifically to prevent the passionate impulses of any given moment from becoming permanent law. The entire architecture of representative democracy assumes there will be time between an idea's emergence and its adoption as policy. Time to debate. Time to consult. Time to reconsider.

That assumption is now under structural pressure from two directions simultaneously. The first is the volume of information. The modern citizen is required to evaluate an exponentially greater volume of information than any previous generation — information that arrives faster, is tailored more precisely to existing beliefs, and is produced by systems explicitly optimised to capture and hold attention. The human brain did not evolve for this environment. We are good at evaluating information when we have time, context, and trusted sources. We are poor at it when we are tired, distracted, emotionally activated, and shown content designed to bypass our critical faculties.

The second pressure is authenticity uncertainty — the growing difficulty of establishing whether a human or a system produced content. Disagreement about facts has always been part of democratic life. Disagreement about whether a voice is genuine or fabricated is a newer and more structurally corrosive problem, because it undermines the epistemological foundations on which democratic debate depends. You cannot debate a person who is not there. You can only ignore a signal whose source you cannot verify.

Democracy runs on informed consent. Informed consent requires the ability to distinguish truth from fabrication. That ability is now the contested terrain.

Some will argue that democracies have survived previous communication disruptions, the printing press, the telegraph, radio, television, the internet, and that they will survive this one too. This argument has merit. It also misses a crucial variable.

In every previous disruption, humans remained the producers of the content moving through new channels. The printing press amplified human speech. What we are encountering now is not simply a faster channel. It is a system that generates content without human authors, at a scale and personalization level that no previous disruption has approximated.

***

WHAT DEMOCRACIES MUST BUILD

The printing press offers instruction here, not as comfort but as a specific historical case study in institutional adaptation. The press appeared in Europe around 1440 and within sixty years had produced millions of books, pamphlets, broadsides, and seditious texts that no existing institution had the capacity to regulate, evaluate, or contextualize.

The Catholic Church, which had served as the primary institution of European knowledge management for over a millennium, found its authority destabilised not because the Church was weak but because its entire architecture — built around the controlled transmission of handwritten manuscripts through institutional channels — was incompatible with the new medium's speed, volume, and decentralization.

The first century after the press saw extraordinary turbulence: the Reformation, the religious wars, the collapse of one kind of European unity and the emergence of another. It also saw the eventual development of new institutions — public libraries, secular universities, free press norms, the gradual emergence of scientific publishing with peer review — that were capable of managing knowledge in the new environment. These institutions took a century to develop, partly because nobody in 1450 knew what institutions would eventually be needed, and partly because institution-building is slow, contested, and expensive.

The pace at which AI-generated content can be created, distributed, and personalised is not comparable to any previous information technology transition. We are dealing with a disruption whose speed is compressed by several orders of magnitude. The institutions that democracies need — that can authenticate sources, contextualize synthetic content, maintain trusted verification infrastructure, build deliberative capacity into the information ecosystem — need to be built in years, not generations.

Some of this is technical. Watermarking, provenance tracking, authentication protocols — there are serious engineering efforts underway to give people better tools for distinguishing human-produced from machine-produced content. These matter. They will not be sufficient. The railroad was eventually governed not primarily through limits on the size of trains but through institutions that built accountability into the system — safety boards, liability frameworks, rate regulation, the slow accumulation of rules that forced the technology to serve public interest rather than simply the interests of those who owned it.

The analogy holds: what will ultimately govern AI is not primarily technical controls on what systems can generate, but social institutions that build the capacity to evaluate, attribute, and hold accountable what those systems do. We need the equivalent of rate regulation and safety oversight — not for trains, but for the systems through which information and decisions now move.

What is needed now is something analogous: the broad development of a capacity to navigate algorithmically curated information environments with the same critical faculty that good readers bring to texts. Call it information literacy, algorithmic literacy, epistemic hygiene — the specific name matters less than the capacity.

And like historical literacy, this capacity cannot simply be legislated into existence. It must be taught, practiced, institutionally supported, and embedded in a culture that values the careful evaluation of evidence over the quick comfort of confirmation.

Sara understood this, sitting in her office after the vote. The legislation had passed. The structural vulnerability had not changed. What she was sitting with was the understanding that a policy victory — even a genuine one — was not the same as the institutional capacity that the moment required. That capacity would take longer to build than any individual piece of legislation could create. It would require sustained investment, sustained political will, and sustained public engagement with questions that were technically complex and politically uncomfortable.

She had not despaired. But she had become clearer-eyed about the scale of what was actually required.

***

WHAT CITIZENS CAN DO

The scale of what democracies need to build — exigent, vast, and pressing against timelines that feel inadequate to the task — can feel paralyzing when you encounter it. Watermarking standards. Authentication infrastructure. Information literacy at scale. Platform accountability frameworks. These are institutional and legislative challenges that no individual can address alone, and the gap between the scale of the problem and the scale of what any individual can do is disorienting.

But the institutional challenges are not the only challenges. They are not even, in some sense, the primary challenges. The institutional challenges will be addressed — slowly, imperfectly, with the usual friction and backsliding — when enough people understand why they matter and insist on them. The understanding comes first. The insisting follows. And both of those are things that individuals do.

There are practices that citizens can develop that are both personally useful and collectively important. The first is what might be called source discipline: the habit of asking, before accepting or sharing a piece of information, where it came from, how it was produced, who benefits from its circulation, and what evidence would count against it. This is not a new practice — journalists and researchers have been doing it for decades — but it has become a citizen practice rather than a professional one, because the information environment that requires it is now universal.

The second is a practice of deliberate slowness. Algorithmic systems are designed to capture and hold attention, which means they are designed to generate reactions before reflection can occur. The deliberate insertion of a pause — before sharing, before commenting, before concluding — is a small act of resistance against the architecture of manipulation.

It is also, in the aggregate, a meaningful one. The disinformation campaigns that have done the most damage have depended on rapid propagation; slowness attenuates them.

The third is the maintenance of epistemic trust relationships — the cultivation and preservation of sources and institutions that you have reason to trust, based on track record rather than alignment with your existing views.

This is harder than it sounds in an environment where algorithmic curation tends to show you content that confirms what you already believe. It requires deliberate attention to voices that present evidence rather than just conclusions, and to institutions that maintain practices of correction and accountability.

Sara had thought about these practices since her legislative experience — not as replacements for institutional reform, but as the ground conditions that made institutional reform possible. The legislation she had passed would have had no path if the legislators who voted for it had not already developed some scepticism about information that arrived without provenance. The capacity for that scepticism was not manufactured by legislation. It was built by individuals, over time, through habits of attention that no one had mandated.

***

Sara's legislation eventually passed. Not by much.

Eighteen months of research. Forty-seven stakeholder groups. Three rounds of public comment. In the end, it squeaked through by eleven votes, half of which Sara later estimated came from legislators who had not fully read the bill but had read enough corrections to the misinformation to feel cautiously reassured.

She sat in her office the evening after the vote. She had won. She understood that it did not feel like winning.

Because what the past three weeks had revealed was not a communications problem with one piece of legislation. It was a structural vulnerability in how democratic societies process information at speed, a vulnerability that would not disappear because this particular vote had gone the right way. The next bill was already in committee. The vulnerability would still be there.

The specific vulnerability is not misinformation as such — democracies have always faced false speech. It is the combination of externalised memory and speed. When the external memory of a civilisation can be seeded with fabrications faster than any institution can evaluate them, and when that seeding can be targeted, personalised, and distributed at scale, the deliberation that democracy requires cannot keep pace. The problem is not that people are believing lies. The problem is that externalised memory, which democratic citizens use to form political judgments, can now be contaminated at a speed the immune system of democratic deliberation was not designed to handle.

The pace at which the vulnerability can be exploited was demonstrated concretely in the days before the Slovak parliamentary election in September 2023. Audio recordings circulated on social media in which the leader of a progressive opposition party appeared to discuss how to manipulate votes and raise beer prices. The recordings were fake — generated by AI audio synthesis and deliberately seeded into social media networks 48 hours before polls opened, in the window after which electoral law prohibits certain kinds of campaign interference.

By the time independent fact-checkers had assessed and rejected the recordings, the election had passed. The deliberative capacity of the democratic system — its ability to evaluate, contextualize, and correct — operated on a timeframe the technology had outrun.

The legislation passed.

The vulnerability remained.

And the next bill was already in committee.

The printing press broke one model of power.

It took a century for new institutions to emerge.

We do not have a century.

We have this decade.

PART III

The Reckoning

When the questions outgrow the answers, clarity becomes an act of courage.

CHAPTER 9

Who Actually Owns the Future?

"It is not the oil that matters. It is the pipe."

— *Ida Tarbell, paraphrased*

The hospital administrator's name was Dr. Kavitha Menon, and she had spent twenty-two years building Greenfield General into something she was quietly proud of. Not a prestigious hospital — they lacked the budget for prestige — but a competent one. They trained junior doctors carefully. Their infection rates ran below national averages. They handled complicated obstetric cases that smaller facilities transferred out. Dr. Menon took satisfaction in what they had built through two decades of careful management of limited resources.

Then the AI diagnostic system contract came up for renewal, and the vendor proposed a price increase of sixty-three percent.

She sat with her CFO and her chief medical officer in the boardroom and looked at the proposal. They modelled the alternatives. They ran the numbers. They asked the clinical teams what would happen if the hospital simply discontinued the contract and returned to pre-integration workflows.

The answer came back in a collective memo from her senior attending physicians — three pages long, clearly the result of considerable disagreement about how to phrase things diplomatically: "We cannot recommend discontinuation. Clinical decision-making in our Emergency Department, ICU, and diagnostic units is now sufficiently integrated with the system that withdrawal would create patient safety risks we are not able to fully quantify."

She read that phrase three times. She knew what physicians meant when they used the phrase "not able to fully quantify" about patient safety. They meant: we believe it would be serious, and we do not want to be the ones to say how serious.

She called the vendor's account manager. His name was Vikas. She had met him twice at industry conferences and found him professionally competent and personally pleasant. He walked her through the rationale for the increase: research and development costs, infrastructure investment, and market validation of the technology's clinical value. The price, he explained, reflected what the system was worth to institutions that had integrated it into their clinical pathways.

He was right. That was exactly what it was worth. That was the problem.

***

STANDARD OIL AND THE INVISIBLE POWER

In 1879, John D. Rockefeller controlled approximately ninety percent of American oil refining capacity. This was remarkable. But what gave his power its particular durability was not his control over refining. It was his control over the infrastructure through which refined oil moved.

By the late 1870s, Standard Oil had established control over a network of pipelines, railroad freight agreements, and storage facilities so comprehensive that a barrel of oil could barely travel from extraction to consumer without touching Standard Oil infrastructure at some point. The oil producers — the people who actually found and pumped the crude — could extract all they wanted. Getting that oil to market at a profitable price required negotiating with Rockefeller's network at every stage.

Ida Tarbell spent nearly five years researching Standard Oil, publishing nineteen instalments in McClure's Magazine between 1902 and 1904 — producing one of the most consequential pieces of investigative journalism in American history. She described what she found in terms that illuminate the specific mechanism of infrastructure power: Standard Oil's dominance was not visible in any single transaction. It was embedded in the structure of the market. Companies that tried to compete did not face an opponent in the marketplace. They faced a world in which the conditions of competition had been set by their opponent before the competition began. The pipelines went where Standard Oil decided they went. The railroads charged what Standard Oil negotiated. The storage facilities were available to whom Standard Oil chose to make them available.

The Sherman Antitrust Act was passed in 1890. Standard Oil was not broken up until 1911. In between, it was investigated, litigated against, and exposed in detail — and it continued to operate, because the infrastructure it controlled had become too embedded in too many supply chains for dismantling to be quick, even when the legal mandate existed.

The lesson is not that Standard Oil was uniquely evil. Rockefeller believed, sincerely if conveniently, that consolidation served the public interest by eliminating inefficiency. The lesson is that infrastructure power compounds and embeds through an inexorable logic of network effects and switching costs — each new dependent makes correction more disruptive, each passing year makes the architecture more entrenched. By the time the resistance organises, the infrastructure has become the precondition for economic activity. You cannot dismantle it without disrupting the activity that depends on it.

***

MAYA, THREE YEARS LATER

Dr. Maya Krishnan had thought many times about the night she watched a system correctly prioritise a subdural hematoma she had ranked third on her differential. She had thought about it not with shame but with a particular quality of sustained attention — the kind you bring to an experience that changed something you had not realised was changeable.

Three years later, she was a senior resident — six months from completing her training, a clinician who had seen enough to have developed the kind of pattern recognition that the system had modelled from twenty million patients. She was, in the specific domain of emergency medicine, genuinely good. She trusted her clinical judgment in ways she had not been able to trust it as a second-year resident.

Her ambivalence was about something else. Something she had taken three years to articulate clearly.

She said it to a colleague over coffee: "I no longer know what I would do without it."

Her colleague — a surgeon named Ravi who had trained before such systems existed — looked at her across his cup. "Does that bother you?"

"It should bother all of us," Maya said. "Not because it's wrong. Because we never made a conscious decision about it. We integrated it because it worked, and now we're dependent in ways we never mapped out. If this specific vendor raised prices by sixty percent tomorrow — I've heard from colleagues in other hospitals that it's happening — we couldn't simply switch. Our workflows, our decision support protocols, and our training of junior residents. All of it has been built around this particular system's outputs."

"Every generation of doctors has said that about some technology," Ravi said. "We couldn't function without imaging. Or anesthesia."

"That's true," Maya said. "But imaging and anesthesia are tools with understood mechanisms. I know what an MRI does and why. What I don't understand is why this system makes the recommendations it makes — what it's actually doing, which means I don't know where it will fail, and I can't prepare for that failure. And Deepak's hospital is now in the same position as mine."

Ravi was quiet for a moment. "What happened to your patient? The one from three years ago?"

"Deepak," Maya said. "He sends me a message every Diwali. He's fine."

"Then something is working."

"Something is working," Maya agreed. "That's not the same as understanding what. And it's not the same as being in control of it."

***

RAJ, RECONSTITUTED

Around the same time that Maya was having this conversation with Ravi, Raj — the strategy consultant who had stared at a forty-seven-second analysis on a Tuesday morning three years earlier — was having a different but related conversation with a client.

Raj had not been displaced. He had done what he had promised himself he would do on the night he lay awake staring at the ceiling: he had figured out what his work actually was, and he had organised himself around that. The research and synthesis layer of his consulting practice was now handled by systems that he and his small team directed and interpreted. The layer he had kept — the interpretive work, the client relationship management, the institutional knowledge, the contextual judgment that came from knowing specific clients in specific industries over long periods — had turned out to be more valuable, not less, as the routine analysis layer became commoditized.

He had reorganised his practice around what he now called "orchestration" — a word he had borrowed from a colleague who used it to describe the work of getting AI-assisted analysis, human judgment, and client decision-making to work together coherently. It was not a word that had existed in consulting vocabulary three years earlier. It described a real function: the capacity to know which questions to ask of the systems, how to evaluate their outputs, where human judgment needed to supplement or override the analysis, and how to translate the combined product into something a specific client could act on.

He was meeting with a new client — a mid-sized logistics company navigating a significant operational restructuring — and the CFO had asked him a question that had become familiar: "What exactly is it that you do that a good AI system can't do?"

Raj had thought about this question long enough that he had a clear answer. "I know what the system doesn't know," he said. "Your regulatory history in the markets you operate in. The specific risk tolerance of your board, which I've spent two years understanding. The reason your operations team reacted the way they did to the last restructuring is that it affects what will work this time. The system can tell you what the data shows. It can't tell you what it means for this company, with this history, with these specific stakeholders."

The CFO was quiet for a moment. "And you can?"

"Better than any system currently available," Raj said. "Not perfectly. But well enough to be worth the difference."

The CFO nodded. They moved on. But Raj drove home that evening thinking about the conversation in the same way he had thought about Deepa's question three years earlier — the client who had asked him, "Is the judgment part still you?" He had arrived, through three years of adaptation, at a place where the answer to both questions was the same: yes, and here is specifically what that means.

***

THE NEW INFRASTRUCTURE

Infrastructure power is different from product power. When a company makes a better product, that power is real but contestable — a competitor can make a different product. When a company controls infrastructure, the power changes in kind. The infrastructure becomes the precondition for participation in economic activity. Access is not one option among others. It is the condition of possibility.

The question we are only beginning to ask — the question Dr. Kavitha Menon was living inside when she looked at that sixty-three percent increase — is whether AI capabilities are becoming infrastructure in this sense. Not optional tools that enhance productivity, but necessary inputs without which participation in certain sectors and roles is no longer viable.

There are signals that this is already happening in domains we rarely examine carefully enough. Legal research. Medical diagnostics. Financial analysis. Credit assessment. Content moderation. Hiring decisions. Educational assessment. These are not peripheral functions. They are the connective tissue of economic and social life. When AI capabilities become integrated into these functions, and when the organisations performing them become dependent on specific AI providers for that integration, the pattern Dr. Menon encountered at Greenfield General may be the pattern that repeats across entire sectors simultaneously.

The concentration of AI capability is already striking. A very small number of institutions control the foundational models underlying the majority of AI applications currently deployed at scale. This concentration reflects genuine technical and economic reality: training frontier AI systems requires computational resources and capital that very few organisations can assemble. The concentration is not a conspiracy. It is a structural consequence of how the technology works.

But the structure of the technology does not determine the structure of its governance. Standard Oil's technical efficiency was real. That did not mean a world in which Standard Oil controlled all American energy infrastructure served the public interest. Efficiency and accountability are different questions, and conflating them — assuming that a system that works well technically is therefore being governed well — is one of the more reliable ways to arrive at a dependency you did not intend to create.

Who builds the infrastructure shapes the world.
Who governs the infrastructure determines what kind of world it becomes.

The concentration-of-power question is not hypothetical outside Western capitals. Sovereign wealth vehicles in the Gulf have committed capital to AI infrastructure at a scale that rivals most governments' defence budgets. National AI programmes across South Asia are explicitly designed to build compute capacity independent of Western hyperscaler dependency — not as a commercial strategy, but as a sovereignty strategy. Several of these programmes have established dedicated national AI authorities with mandates that go well beyond research — bodies designed to govern, direct, and in some cases own the infrastructure layer itself. The governments moving fastest in this space are not primarily concerned with regulatory compliance frameworks. They are concerned with a simpler and more consequential question: who controls the infrastructure on which their economies and institutions will run? That question is being answered right now, in rooms that the Brussels AI Act conversation does not reach, with an urgency that the pace of European regulatory deliberation does not match.

That question — who controls the infrastructure — is the infrastructure version of the question this book has been asking all along. We did not build artificial intelligence. We built civilisation's external memory. And as with every previous form of external memory, from the Library of Alexandria to the printing press to the internet, what is built around it — the institutions, the governance, the ownership structures — determines whose civilisation it serves.

***

WHAT A NEW OWNERSHIP MODEL MIGHT LOOK LIKE

The concentration of AI capability in a small number of private entities is not inevitable. It is the outcome of specific choices — about investment, about intellectual property law, about the public goods that governments did and did not fund, about the regulatory frameworks that were or were not built during the period when the technology was developing rapidly, and most people in government had not yet understood what was developing.

Different choices are possible. They are increasingly being made, in fragments, in different jurisdictions and domains. Some countries are investing in publicly funded AI research and development at a scale that creates genuine alternatives to exclusively private infrastructure. Some sectors — healthcare, education, public administration — are beginning to negotiate the terms on which they adopt private AI systems rather than simply accepting whatever terms vendors offer. Some municipalities are building shared data infrastructure that allows AI systems serving public purposes to be trained on data that remains under democratic control.

None of these are sufficient on their own. Together, they represent the beginning of an institutional response to a concentration problem that is real and that has real consequences. The question is whether the response will be fast enough and comprehensive enough to preserve the possibility of meaningful alternatives before the network effects of early concentrated adoption make genuine alternatives impossible.

The monopoly is not complete. The infrastructure is not yet entirely private. The data commons — the accumulated knowledge of human civilisation, the scientific literature, the historical record, the cultural production — was not created by private entities and does not belong to them, though they have been its primary beneficiaries in the current phase of AI development. Asserting meaningful public interest in the governance of systems trained on public knowledge is not nationalisation. It is the enforcement of a legitimate claim that has not yet been adequately articulated or pursued.

Ida Tarbell did not stop Standard Oil by herself. Her journalism exposed the problem and made it impossible for the public to remain unaware of it. The response to Standard Oil — the Sherman Antitrust Act, its eventual enforcement, the breakup of the monopoly — required legislative action, executive will, and decades of sustained public pressure. Tarbell's contribution was to make the problem visible in a way that demanded response.

We are at a similar moment: the problem is becoming visible. The response is not yet adequate to the scale of the problem. The visibility is the necessary precondition for the response. Without it, change is not possible. With it, change is not guaranteed — but it becomes possible.

The counter-example to Standard Oil's governance problem is Estonia, which spent two decades quietly building the answer to a question most governments had not yet asked: how do you govern AI infrastructure if you don't own it? Estonia's X-Road system, developed incrementally from 2001 onward, is a national data exchange layer that allows government agencies, banks, hospitals, and private companies to share data without any central repository. Ninety-nine percent of government services are available digitally. Citizens and organisations have the right to see who has queried their data. No single entity — including the state — owns the data; it stays with the originating institution. The architecture was designed to prevent the kind of dependency capture that Standard Oil had perfected. By building decentralised data ownership into the infrastructure itself, Estonia ensured that no single private or public actor could achieve the leverage that comes from controlling the data layer. The result is not a utopia. It is a country where the infrastructure question was answered before it became a crisis. That is not an accident. It is what deliberate, early institutional design looks like when it works.

***

RAHUL'S QUALITY CONTROL

Three years after the goodbye drinks in October, Rahul had a position in a smaller organisation — one of the companies in the sector he had spent eleven years in, now operating with AI-assisted quality control systems that had been implemented in the eighteen months before he joined. He had not been part of the implementation. He had arrived into a system already in place.

What he discovered, in the first few months, was that nobody at the organisation had a clear picture of what the AI system was actually optimizing for. The system had been implemented by a previous team, trained on historical data, and deployed with a set of documentation that described its technical specifications more clearly than its behavioural tendencies. The people who had implemented it had moved on. The people who operated it trusted its outputs without, in most cases, understanding why it produced them.

This was not malice. It was the ordinary entropy of institutional knowledge in organisations that moves quickly. The system had been implemented, it had produced adequate-looking results, and the detailed understanding of what it was doing and why had not been sufficiently documented or preserved. The people now running the organisation were dependent on a system they did not fully understand.

Rahul recognised the situation because he had been on the other side of it in his previous position — he had been part of teams that had implemented systems and moved on, leaving less documentation than would have been ideal because there had not been time. He had not thought carefully then about what that meant for the people who came after him. He thought carefully about it now.

He spent four months building what the organisation called a "system audit" — a process for regularly reviewing what the AI quality control system was actually flagging and why, comparing its outputs to human quality assessments, identifying systematic patterns in its errors, and maintaining a living document of what was known and unknown about its behaviour. It was not glamorous work. It was foundational. It was the difference between operating infrastructure you understood and operating infrastructure you were hoping worked as intended.

The audit produced several findings that changed how the system was used. Two categories of defect that the system consistently underweighted — which had seemed fine in the historical data because they were rare, but which appeared frequently enough in the current production environment to matter — were added to the human review protocol. One category where the system's performance significantly exceeded human accuracy was identified, and the human review protocol was adjusted to allocate less time to it.

The infrastructure had not changed. The understanding of it had. And the understanding made the dependency a managed one rather than an unexamined one. That, Rahul thought, was not a small thing. It was the kind of thing that distinguished an organisation that would notice when its systems failed from one that would not notice until the failure had already compounded.

***

Dr. Menon signed the renewal. There was no realistic alternative.

Maya continued working alongside the system she could not explain and could not work without.

Raj rebuilt his practice around what the systems could not do.

Not without difficulty. But with clarity.

The tools became infrastructure.

Infrastructure became a dependency.

Dependency became invisible.

And invisible systems are the ones that govern most completely.

The question of who owns the future is not a philosophical abstraction.

It is being answered right now —

in investment decisions and product roadmaps

made by a small number of people

in rooms most of us have never visited.

This is not inevitable.

It is a choice.

The question is whether we will make it consciously or have it made for us.

WHAT SHARED INFRASTRUCTURE LOOKS LIKE

The history of public goods offers a guide to what shared AI infrastructure could look like, though the parallel requires care. Electricity was not made public everywhere — most of the world's electrical grids are operated by a mixture of public and private entities, with different regulatory structures, different ownership models, and different accountability mechanisms. What matters is not the ownership structure in the abstract but the accountability structure: who is responsible for what, how failures are addressed, and whether the system serves broad interests or narrow ones.

Applied to AI infrastructure, this suggests a set of questions that are more useful than the binary of "public" versus "private." Who controls the training data? Who decides what the training objectives are? Who can audit the system's outputs and on what basis? Who bears the costs when the system fails, and through what mechanism? Who has the right to opt out, and under what conditions? These questions do not have universal answers — the right answers for a healthcare diagnostic system are different from the right answers for a consumer recommendation engine.

But the questions themselves, asked systematically, constitute an accountability framework that is considerably more useful than the current default of leaving all of these decisions to whoever built the system.

Some countries are beginning to develop regulatory frameworks along these lines. The European Union's AI Act attempts to categorise systems by risk level and impose requirements commensurate with that risk. The United States is developing sector-specific guidance through agencies with existing regulatory authority. India, with one of the largest user populations for AI systems, is working through its own approach. None of these frameworks is yet adequate — they are moving faster than regulatory frameworks typically move, which is to say they are moving at about a third of the speed required to keep pace with the technology.

The gap between the speed of deployment and the speed of governance is itself a form of choice. It reflects decisions — made by technology companies, by governments, by investors, by the public — about what priorities matter. A society that deployed a new pharmaceutical at the pace that AI systems are being deployed, without the equivalent of clinical trials and regulatory review, would be recognised as having made a catastrophically irresponsible decision. That we have not yet developed the equivalent recognition for AI deployment is not evidence that the risks are smaller. It is evidence that we have not yet developed the vocabulary and institutional reflexes to take them seriously.

Three years after her first encounter with the diagnostic system, Maya sat in a committee meeting that had the particular quality of all important institutional work: unglamorous, technical, and poorly attended. The room had seven people in it. It should have had fifteen. The agenda item was a proposal to expand a respiratory triage AI to two additional wards, and the vendor's presentation had been polished and confident and had, Maya had noticed, said almost nothing about what happened when the system was wrong.

She had asked the question before the presentation was finished. "What does the error distribution look like across patient demographics?" The vendor representative had answered with aggregate accuracy statistics. Maya had asked again, more specifically: in the patients where the system's confidence was highest and it was still incorrect, was there a pattern in who those patients were? The room went quiet in the particular way that rooms go quiet when someone has asked a question that the presenter was not prepared for and that the other people in the room now realise they should have asked themselves.

The answer, after three follow-up exchanges over two weeks, was yes: the system had been trained on data that underrepresented elderly patients with multiple comorbidities, and its confident wrong answers clustered in exactly that population. The expansion was delayed. A retraining requirement was added to the contract. Maya had not stopped the technology — she had never wanted to stop it. She had required it to be honest about where it failed before it was permitted to fail in new places. That distinction was the entire point of the committee.

This is what governance actually looks like — not as legislation passed in chambers, but as practice maintained in rooms. The future of accountability around AI systems is being built in meetings like this one, by people like Maya who show up, ask the precise question, and insist on the answer. The role is unglamorous. The meetings are long. The institutional capacity being built in those rooms — the capacity to exercise meaningful oversight over systems that are powerful — is something that no law, however well-drafted, can substitute for.

CHAPTER 10

Most AI Ethics Conversations Are Superficial

"The peculiar evil of silencing the expression of an opinion is that it is robbing the human race — those who dissent from the opinion, still more than those who hold it."

— John Stuart Mill, On Liberty, 1859

The ethics board had fourteen members. Their first meeting lasted three and a half hours. There was a facilitator, a prepared agenda, and a catered lunch. The members included a moral philosopher from a respected university, a retired appeals court judge, two civil society representatives, a bioethicist, a former government minister, and several technology executives who had volunteered for the board because, as one of them explained in his opening remarks, "we believe responsible development of this technology requires diverse ethical perspectives."

Ananya Pillai had been invited as an external legal consultant — her role was to advise on liability questions, on what the company's legal exposure might look like across various harm scenarios.

She sat through three and a half hours with the careful attention she had brought to every professional engagement since her first week at the law firm, when a senior partner had told her that the most important skill in legal practice was listening to what people were not saying.

What she heard, in that elegant boardroom, was an extended conversation about the ethics of AI that never once addressed the question of what would actually change as a result of the board's recommendations.

The philosopher gave a thoughtful forty-minute presentation distinguishing consequentialist and deontological approaches to algorithmic harm. The judge raised procedural due process concerns. The civil society representatives discussed community consultation. The bioethicist drew parallels to clinical trials ethics. The conversation was technically substantive. These were intelligent people who had thought seriously about genuine questions.

But at no point during the three and a half hours did anyone ask: "What is the enforcement mechanism if the company's systems cause harm despite our ethical guidelines?" At no point did anyone ask: "Which specific product decisions does this board have authority to modify?" At no point did anyone ask: "What happens when our recommendations conflict with the commercial roadmap?"

After the meeting, walking to the elevator, Ananya fell into step with the moral philosopher — a gentle man named Dr. Acharya who had been visibly engaged throughout the discussion.

"What did you make of it?" she asked him.

He was quiet for a moment. "Intellectually stimulating," he said finally. "Practically..." Another pause. "I'm not certain what the board's actual authority is."

"Neither am I," Ananya said. "And I was hired to advise on liability."

***

THE PLAZA HOTEL, 1953

In December 1953, executives from the major American tobacco companies gathered at the Plaza Hotel in New York City. The meeting had been called in response to a crisis: a series of scientific studies, most prominently a paper in the British Medical Journal, had established a statistical link between cigarette smoking and lung cancer. The evidence was not yet overwhelming — scientific consensus builds gradually — but it was becoming increasingly difficult to dismiss.

The executives engaged Hill & Knowlton, a public relations firm, to develop a strategy. What they developed together became one of the most consequential and most carefully documented corporate communications campaigns in history — a template that would be deployed, in various forms, across industries for decades.

The strategy was not to deny the cancer link outright. That would have been too easily falsifiable as the evidence accumulated. The strategy was subtler: to manufacture the appearance of scientific controversy where a genuine consensus was forming — a tendentious deployment of the form of scientific inquiry without its substance, the procedures of doubt without the honest search for truth that those procedures were designed to serve. To find and fund researchers willing to raise questions, introduce doubt, and call for more study. To create the impression that the science was "not settled" — and to sustain that impression for as long as possible.

A 1969 internal tobacco industry document, later made public through litigation, stated the strategic objective with startling directness: "Doubt is our product, since it is the best means of competing with the body of fact that exists in the mind of the general public."

Doubt is our product.

The campaign worked for two decades. Smoking rates remained high through the 1950s and 1960s, even as the scientific evidence against cigarettes mounted. Congressional hearings were held. The Surgeon General's landmark report was issued in 1964. And still the industry delayed meaningful regulatory response — through litigation, lobbying, the sustained manufacture of scientific uncertainty, and the basic human tendency to believe what we want to believe when the alternative is uncomfortable and expensive.

The tobacco playbook has since been deployed across industries facing adverse scientific findings: the fossil fuel industry's response to climate science; pharmaceutical companies' selective disclosure of clinical trial data; the food industry's management of research on sugar and metabolic disease. The specific tactics vary. The structure is consistent: manufacture uncertainty, demand more study, fund sympathetic researchers, delay consensus, and in the years purchased by that delay, extract maximum value from the status quo.

The lesson for AI ethics is not that technology companies are the tobacco industry. The lesson is that ethics-as-performance is structurally available as a strategy whenever accountability mechanisms are weak — and that the gap between genuine ethical commitment and its performed simulacrum can be very wide and very difficult to close from the outside.

***

THE GAP FILES

In the four years since joining the law firm, Ananya's practice had evolved in ways she had not anticipated. She had arrived expecting corporate work. She had ended up spending an increasing portion of her time on questions at the intersection of law, technology, and harm: who was responsible when an algorithmic hiring system produced discriminatory outcomes? What was the standard of care when a medical AI made an error? How should courts think about causation when a decision was made by a system that no individual human fully understood?

These arrived as actual clients with actual injuries, navigating legal systems built for a world in which a human decision-maker could be identified, their reasoning examined, and their duty of care assessed.

What Ananya had learned across dozens of cases was that the gap between what companies said about their AI ethics and what those statements meant in practice was, more often than not, very wide.

She had started keeping a folder she called "the gap files" — cases where companies had publicly committed to ethical principles that their deployed systems appeared to violate. Not because the companies were lying, necessarily. Because the connection between the ethics conversation and the engineering decisions had never been made structurally binding, the two processes operated in parallel, occasionally referenced each other, and had no formal mechanism of integration.

She described one case to her mentor, the senior partner who had advised her, on her first day, to listen for what people were not saying. The case involved a company whose AI hiring tool had been producing outcomes that systematically disadvantaged candidates from certain demographic groups. The company had an ethics board. The company had published ethical AI principles. The ethics board had not reviewed the hiring tool's deployment decision. The ethical AI principles did not specify an enforcement mechanism.

"When did the company discover the pattern?" her mentor asked.

"Eighteen months after deployment," Ananya said. "Through an external audit commissioned by a civil society organisation. Not through their internal processes."

He nodded slowly. "And the ethics board?"

"Was not informed of the audit results until they were public," Ananya said.

Her mentor was quiet for a moment. "What you're describing," he said finally, "is the difference between principles and constraints. Principles describe what you aspire to. Constraints determine what you can and cannot do. The company had principles. It did not have constraints. The ethics board was an aspirational structure, not an accountability structure."

"And the legal system?" Ananya asked.

"The legal system," he said, "is trying to apply frameworks built for individual decision-makers to systems that distribute decision-making across multiple actors and multiple layers. It's struggling. That's why the cases that come to us are so difficult." He looked at her. "That's also why the ethics conversation and the legal conversation need to happen in the same room, with the same urgency, rather than in parallel tracks that rarely intersect."

***

SARA AND THE GOVERNANCE ROOM

Sara Nair had been following the AI ethics debate from her position in public policy with increasing frustration — a frustration she kept mostly private, because openly frustrated policy advisors are rarely effective ones. But in conversations she trusted, she had begun to say clearly what she was seeing.

"The problem," she said to a colleague one afternoon, "is that the ethics conversation is happening in the wrong rooms. Company boardrooms, academic conferences, media panels. Those aren't bad rooms for ethics conversations. But they're not the rooms where product decisions get made."

"Where does the real work happen?" her colleague asked.

"Engineering meetings," Sara said. "Investor calls. Roadmap planning sessions. The places where specific decisions are made about what gets built, for whom, and how. Those rooms have almost no formal connection to the ethics conversations happening in the other rooms. They reference the same documents. They use the same vocabulary. But the decisions flow from different logics, on different timescales, with different accountability structures."

She had spent months studying what governance structures actually closed that gap. What she found was that the most effective precedents came from regulatory contexts where external accountability was built in from the start: aviation safety, pharmaceutical approval, and financial auditing. Industries where the consequences of failure were severe, visible, and attributable. Where a crash, a contaminated drug batch, or a fraudulent audit created pressure for accountability that market forces alone had not created.

The systems of oversight in those industries had been built, often after catastrophic failures, because the status quo had proven inadequate. The question for AI governance was whether the field would follow the same pattern — learning primarily from disasters — or whether the evidence available now was sufficient to build accountability structures before disasters made them unavoidable.

Sara was not optimistic about the timeline. She was experienced enough to know that robust regulatory systems rarely get built before the crisis they would have prevented. But she was also experienced enough to know that this was a reason to work faster, not a reason to accept the outcome.

***

WHAT REAL ETHICS REQUIRES

The distinction between substantive ethics and performed ethics is not a distinction between sincere and insincere actors.

Most of the people involved in AI ethics conversations are sincere. The distinction is architectural: substantive ethics requires that ethical commitments be connected, through concrete mechanisms, to actual decisions about what gets built, deployed, and governed. Performed ethics requires only that the conversation happen.

Real ethics, in any domain, has three components that most AI ethics processes currently lack. The first is enforcement — a commitment that cannot be enforced is an aspiration, and aspirations are not the same as commitments. The second is accountability — someone must be identifiable, reachable, and responsible when harm occurs, and that responsibility must be established before harm occurs rather than negotiated afterward. The third is participation — the communities most affected by AI systems must be present in the rooms where decisions about those systems are made, not as afterthoughts in consultation processes but as stakeholders with real influence.

These three requirements are not technically complex. They are institutionally difficult. They require organisations to accept constraints on their freedom of action. They require regulators to move in the face of uncertainty. They require companies to prioritise accountability over narrative management. None of these are comfortable. All of them are necessary.

Ethics that change nothing except the reputation of those practicing it is not ethics. It is a mirror held at a flattering angle.

WHAT ACCOUNTABILITY ACTUALLY REQUIRES

The tobacco industry's strategy from 1953 onward offers a clarifying example of what ethics looks like when it is entirely performative. The industry did not openly deny that cigarettes caused cancer. They created a research institute that published papers emphasizing uncertainty, sponsored conferences that mixed genuine scientific inquiry with industry-favorable conclusions, and developed a sophisticated public communications strategy that kept the public in a state of managed confusion for decades. The tobacco executives who ran this strategy were intelligent people. Most of them were not unintelligent about the underlying facts. They chose, collectively and institutionally, to pursue the appearance of scientific engagement while working to prevent the implications of the science from being acted on.

The parallel with contemporary AI ethics processes is not perfect. The AI industry contains many people of genuine good faith who are seriously trying to address real problems. But the structural incentive that produces tobacco-industry behaviour — the pressure to maintain commercial operations while appearing to address the risks of those operations — is present in the AI industry in ways that should make us sceptical of processes that produce ethical-sounding statements without enforceable commitments.

The ethics gap is, in part, a memory problem. The principles that governance conversations produce — the stated values, the commitments, the frameworks — are stored in external memory. They exist in documents and guidelines, and mission statements, accessible to anyone. What external memory cannot do is close the gap between a principle in a document and a decision in an engineering meeting. That closure is a human act, requiring human accountability structures. It cannot be offloaded to the system that is supposed to embody the principle.

COMPAS — Correctional Offender Management Profiling for Alternative Sanctions — is a risk assessment tool used in US courts to predict the likelihood that a defendant will reoffend. A 2016 ProPublica investigation found that the system falsely flagged Black defendants as high-risk at roughly twice the rate of white defendants. The company's response was to produce its own statistical analysis showing parity on a different metric — overall accuracy across racial groups was similar. Both analyses were technically correct. They measured different things. The company had satisfied itself that the ethics conversation had been adequately engaged with. The people disproportionately labelled high-risk had not been protected by that engagement. The gap between the ethics process and the real-world outcome was exactly what the performed-ethics pattern predicts.

Real accountability requires specificity. "We take safety seriously" is not an accountability commitment — it is a positioning statement. "Our systems will not be deployed in contexts where failure would cause irreversible harm without the following specific human oversight mechanisms in place, and the following independent body and subject will audit violations of this commitment to the following penalties" is an accountability commitment. The distance between these two statements is the distance between performed ethics and substantive ethics.

What Ananya was building — the habit of noticing when the system's output diverged from contextual reality, the capacity to interrogate that divergence, the willingness to act on her judgment — was a micro-version of the accountability practice that institutions need to build at scale. She was not blindly trusting the system. She was not blindly rejecting it. She was maintaining the gap — the evaluative space between the system's output and the decision — in which human judgment still lived and functioned. Institutions need the equivalent of that gap: not rejection of AI systems, but the preserved capacity to evaluate them, question them, override them, and be accountable for the decisions that result.

The legal term for this is due diligence. The ethical term for it is responsibility. The practical implication is that organisations deploying AI systems must maintain human expertise sufficient to meaningfully evaluate those systems, which means not deploying systems faster than their oversight capacity can develop, not outsourcing the entire analytical layer to tools whose outputs no one on staff fully understands, and not treating the existence of a system as a substitute for the judgment that the system was supposed to assist.

A 2024 ruling in a Canadian court made this principle legally concrete. Air Canada had deployed a chatbot to handle customer service inquiries, including questions about bereavement fares. A customer was told by the chatbot that reduced fares could be claimed retroactively after a family bereavement — information that was incorrect. Air Canada's defence was that the chatbot was "a separate legal entity" and that the company was not responsible for statements it had made. The court rejected this argument. Air Canada was responsible for its chatbot's outputs in the same way it was responsible for any other statement made by its agents. The verdict was narrow and specific. Its implication was broad: deploying a system to interact with customers or stakeholders does not transfer responsibility to the system. The institution remains accountable for what the system says and does. The accountability gap that performance ethics exploits is, it turns out, also a legal risk.

***

MOVING FROM CONVERSATION TO COMMITMENT

Ananya, eighteen months after the cross-border transaction incident, was asked to serve on an internal working group on AI governance at her firm. The working group had been established in response to a client inquiry about the firm's approach to responsible AI use — not a regulatory requirement, not a crisis response, but a proactive question from a client sophisticated enough to ask it.

What she found, when she began the work, was that the firm had extensive documentation about its approach to AI — principles, guidelines, value statements — and almost no mechanisms for enforcing any of it. The principles said that human judgment would remain central to client advice. There was no process for ensuring that was actually happening. The guidelines said that AI-generated analysis would be reviewed before it was presented to clients. The review was nominal in practice — a quick scan, not a genuine evaluation.

The gap between the principles and the practice was not the result of bad faith. It was the result of the ordinary pressure of professional life: the deals moved fast, the clients were impatient, the review process was time-consuming, and nobody with authority had decided that the time-consumption was worth it. The principles had been written in a moment of calm reflection. They were being ignored in the moments of pressure when they mattered most.

Ananya's working group spent six months producing a set of specific, auditable commitments — not principles, but procedures. Not "human judgment will remain central" but "every AI-generated analysis presented to a client will be reviewed by a named individual who signs off that they have evaluated the output against the specific context of this client's situation." Not "we will use AI responsibly" but "we will track the cases where our AI system's output was overridden by human judgment, and we will review those cases quarterly to understand what the system is missing."

The procedures were annoying to implement. They slowed certain things down. Several partners pushed back. But they were, in the assessment of the client who had asked the original question, the first AI governance framework they had seen from a professional services firm that appeared to be genuinely trying to hold itself accountable rather than simply trying to appear accountable.

This is the distance between performed ethics and substantive ethics. It is not a large distance in conceptual terms. It is a very large distance in institutional terms because crossing it requires accepting constraints on freedom of action that are real, visible, and occasionally inconvenient. Organizations that are willing to accept those constraints are, in Ananya's experience, rare. They are also, in her observation, the ones that clients actually trust.

Sara, whose legislative work had produced a framework that attempted to impose analogous constraints at the sectoral level, understood the same dynamic from the other direction. The hardest part of writing accountability legislation is not the technical definitions. It is creating the conditions under which enforcement is actually possible, where the violations are detectable, where the responsible parties are identifiable, where the penalties are meaningful rather than nominal, and where the political will to actually enforce exists. None of these conditions appears automatically. All of them require sustained institutional effort.

***

WHAT THE ANANYA STORY MEANS AT SCALE

The story of Ananya's working group matters not as an example of a company doing AI ethics unusually well, though it was that. It matters as a description of a pattern that scales, slowly and unevenly, through professional communities that talk to each other and observe each other's practices.

Professional communities are accountability structures. Not efficient ones, not always reliable ones, but real ones. Lawyers operate within a profession that has formal accountability mechanisms — bar associations, disciplinary procedures, malpractice liability — and informal ones: reputation within peer communities, the judgment of colleagues whose opinion matters, and the long-term effects of how you are known to practice. These informal mechanisms are often more effective than the formal ones at actually shaping behaviour, because they operate continuously rather than only when formal processes are triggered.

The barriers are real and familiar. The incentive structures in many technology organisations reward speed and scale far more reliably than they reward accountability. The professional culture is young. But every professional culture was once as new and undeveloped as this one — medicine, law, engineering all went through periods in which their norms were contested and their accountability mechanisms weak, established slowly through the accumulated weight of individual decisions. The process is underway. Whether it reaches adequate maturity in adequate time is the open question.

CHAPTER 11

Dharma, Not Drama

"Better is one's own dharma, though imperfectly performed, than the dharma of another well performed."

— *Bhagavad Gita, 18.47*

The night before the battle, Arjuna could not sleep.

He walked to the edge of the camp and stood at the boundary where the firelight ended, and the darkness of Kurukshetra began. Both armies had withdrawn for the night. The plain was vast and still. In the distance, beyond the enemy fires, Arjuna could see the silhouettes of tents, the dark shapes of horses, the occasional movement of a guard making his rounds. Men who were, many of them, his cousins. His teachers. His childhood friends' fathers. Men he had eaten with, trained alongside, celebrated victories with through fifteen years of shared history.

He had not expected to feel this way. He was Arjuna — the greatest archer of his age, a warrior who had never flinched from battle, who had fought gods and demons and mortal enemies without wavering. Courage was not his problem.

The problem was simpler and more terrible: standing here, in the darkness, in the specific silence of the night before a catastrophic thing, he could see both sides clearly. His cousins had stolen the kingdom through treachery. The injustice was real. The cause was just. He had rehearsed this reasoning many times, in the council chambers and on the march here, and it had held.

But standing at the edge of the camp, looking at the fires on the other side of the field, Arjuna could not hold onto the clarity that had seemed obvious at distance. What was clear in the planning room became complicated when you could see the specific silhouettes of the people who would die tomorrow.

He went back to Krishna.

Krishna was awake — he always seemed to be awake — sitting at the front of the chariot with his arms resting on his knees, watching the darkness with the particular stillness of someone who was not troubled by what it contained. He looked at Arjuna's face and said nothing for a long moment.

"I cannot do it," Arjuna said. He gestured toward the enemy lines. "I see Bhishma there. And Drona — my own teacher. My kinsmen. If I kill them, what does the kingdom matter? What does any of it matter?"

Krishna was quiet.

"You grieve for those who should not be grieved for," he said at last, "and you speak words of wisdom. But the wise grieve neither for the living nor for the dead."

"That is very easy to say," Arjuna said. His voice was more bitter than he had intended.

"It is not easy," Krishna said. "It is the hardest thing. You are treating this as a question about outcomes — who will live, who will die, what the kingdom will look like afterward. But that is the wrong question."

"What is the right question?"

"What does your dharma require?"

Arjuna looked at him. "I am a warrior. A kshatriya. My dharma requires me to fight when the cause is just."

"Yes," Krishna said. "And you have established that the cause is just. So why are you not fighting?"

"Because I will have to kill people I love."

"Yes," Krishna said again. And he waited.

Arjuna had no answer. Krishna let the silence expand until it became something other than silence — until it became a pressure, a question not being asked aloud that Arjuna could feel pressing against the edges of his understanding.

"Your attachment to outcomes," Krishna said finally, "is the thing that has paralysed you. You are not calculating whether to fight. You are calculating whether the fight will produce a world you find acceptable. But that calculation is not yours to make. Your domain is the action. The outcome belongs to something larger than any of us."

"So I should simply act?" Arjuna said. "Regardless of the consequences?"

"You should act according to what your nature, your role, and your duty require. Not for the reward. Not from fear of a particular outcome. From the recognition that this is what you are here to do. Perform the action. Release the fruit. This is the teaching at the heart of everything."

Arjuna was quiet for a long time. Then he said: "And if I act from duty, and the outcome is terrible?"

"Then the outcome is terrible," Krishna said. "And you will have acted rightly. These two things can coexist. In fact, they must coexist — because if we only act rightly when we can guarantee a good outcome, we will rarely act at all. And the world needs action, not paralysis, from those who understand what is at stake."

The conversation that followed — preserved as the Bhagavad Gita — ranged across metaphysics, the nature of the self, the structure of the cosmos. But its core insight was this: Arjuna's paralysis did not come from cowardice. It came from the belief that his actions needed to produce a specific, guaranteed outcome to be morally justified. When Krishna released him from that belief, when he taught him to act from duty rather than from the desire for a particular result, Arjuna could move again.

This story is three thousand years old. It has been interpreted in every century since. But it seems to me, standing in our particular historical moment, unusually relevant.

***

THE ROOT OF THE WORD

The Sanskrit word dharma comes from the root dhr — to hold, to sustain, to support. This etymology is not abstract. It captures the essence of the concept.

Dharma is what holds things together.

In individual terms, it refers to the duties and behaviours appropriate to one's particular role, nature, and stage of life — the conduct that sustains a person's integrity across time. In social terms, it refers to the principles and structures that sustain a community's coherence. In cosmic terms, it refers to the order that sustains the universe itself. The word operates simultaneously at all three levels — individual, social, cosmic — which is why it resists translation. English has no single word that means personal duty and social law and cosmic order all at once.

The Gita's central instruction — act according to your dharma, without attachment to the fruits of action — is often misread as passive or fatalistic. It is in fact the opposite. It is a teaching about where to anchor your sense of worth when external rewards become unreliable. The worker who has anchored their identity in the work itself — in the genuine application of skill to genuine problems — is less devastated by the reorganisation of the market than the worker who has anchored it in the specific reward the market previously offered.

More broadly, the detachment from outcome is not indifference. It is freedom — freedom from the paralysis that comes when we refuse to act until we can guarantee results. Arjuna's paralysis is the paralysis of every person who has looked at a large, complex, high-stakes problem and concluded that they cannot act on it because they cannot control how it ends. Krishna's answer does not guarantee good outcomes. It is a release from the demand for such a guarantee as a precondition for action.

This distinction matters enormously when we think about technology and its governance. Because one of the most common responses to the scale of AI's challenges — the inequality, the democratic vulnerability, the concentration of power, the governance gaps — is a paralysis that looks very much like Arjuna's at the edge of *Kurukshetra.*

The systems are so vast. The stakes so high. The outcomes so uncertain. The people with actual power to change things so remote. And so the rest of us stand at the boundary of the field, watching the fires on both sides, and accumulate reasons why action is premature, impossible, or unlikely to produce the outcomes we would prefer.

Dharma says: that is the wrong frame. Act in accordance with your role and situation. Act with whatever skill and care your nature allows. Act now, on the things within your reach. Leave the outcomes to what will come.

***

WHAT DHARMA LOOKS LIKE IN PRACTICE

I have spent a significant portion of this book describing structural problems — infrastructure dependencies, democratic vulnerabilities, governance gaps, concentrations of power. These are real. They matter. But a book that describes structural problems and then tells its readers that the problems are structural has done only half its job, at best.

The question dharma puts to structural analysis is: given this specific situation, what does your particular role require of you?

For the engineer building AI systems, dharma requires building with the care of someone who understands the stakes — and refusing to build what your judgment tells you will cause harm, regardless of what the product roadmap says. This is not comfortable. It may cost you professionally. But the engineer who says "I built what I was asked to build" when the outcomes are harmful has not discharged their responsibility. They have simply distributed it upward. Dharma does not accept that distribution.

For the executive deploying these systems, dharma requires taking accountability for outcomes, not just processes. This means funding not only the development of capability but the rigorous, independent understanding of its effects. It means being willing to slow a product roadmap when evidence of harm is present but commercially inconvenient. The executive who builds accountability structures only after a crisis has used the crisis as a learning mechanism that could have been avoided.

For the citizen whose life is being shaped by these systems, dharma requires remaining a participant — not a passive consumer of technology's outputs, but someone who asks questions, expresses preferences, supports governance that creates real accountability, and refuses the comfortable resignation of "it's too complicated for me to understand." Complexity is not an exemption from participation. It is the reason participation is harder and therefore more important.

For the parent watching a child grow up in this world, dharma requires helping that child develop not technical fluency with the systems but the human wisdom to evaluate what the systems tell them — to know when to trust and when to question, to understand that they are agents in this world and not merely its subjects. Suhana's question — why does the phone need to know things? — is exactly the question a parent's dharma requires them to help their child keep asking.

For the policymaker who has authority over governance structures, dharma requires using that authority — not mistaking the difficulty of the regulatory challenge for a reason to defer indefinitely. Governance that arrives only after the crisis it was meant to prevent has served the status quo, not the public. The policymaker who acts before achieving pellucid certainty, from their best judgment of what the situation requires, is practicing dharma. The one who waits for certainty that will never arrive is practicing something else.

***

DHARMA AS ALIGNMENT

The word "alignment" has been adopted by the AI research community to describe the challenge of ensuring that AI systems pursue goals beneficial to humans, rather than proxy objectives that diverge in harmful ways. This is described as a technical problem, and it is — it involves specific challenges in training methodology, evaluation, and system design that serious researchers are working on.

But alignment is, at its core, a dharmic concept. What dharma asks of individuals, alignment asks of systems: not merely that they be capable, but that their capability be oriented toward what holds things together rather than what breaks them apart. A system that is technically excellent but serves concentrated interests at the expense of distributed wellbeing is not aligned in the dharmic sense. Its capability is pointed in the wrong direction. The dhr root is not satisfied by power alone. It is satisfied by power that sustains.

The challenge for a civilisation that has externalised its memory is that the memory itself has no dharma. It holds what it was trained on. What is right, what sustains, what holds things together — these are not properties of memory. They are properties of the judgment that memory is supposed to serve. Dharma cannot be offloaded. It must be practised by specific people in specific roles at the specific moments their position makes available to them. That is what alignment, in the deepest sense, means.

This is the bridge between the ancient text and the contemporary challenge. The question Arjuna faced was not whether to be capable — he was already the greatest archer of his age. The question was whether his capability would be oriented toward what his role and duty required, toward what held the social order together, or toward his personal preference for a world without painful choices.

The question we face is analogous. We have built tools of extraordinary capability. The question is not whether to use them — they are already in use, embedded in systems we depend on, shaping decisions that affect billions of people. The question is whether we will use them in ways that sustain — that hold together the social fabric, the democratic institutions, the human capacity for self-determination — or in ways that serve narrower purposes without regard for what they may be quietly breaking.

What makes this a dharmic question rather than merely a technical one is that it cannot be answered by optimization. You cannot define "sustain" precisely enough to write a loss function for it. You cannot measure "what holds things together" with sufficient precision to train a system on it. These are human judgments — contextual, value-laden, dependent on an understanding of what the situation actually requires of specific people in specific roles — and they require the human exercise of something the ancient text called duty and modern language might call responsibility.

The people who will navigate this transition well are not the ones who are most technically sophisticated or most financially resourced. They are the ones who have maintained the capacity for this kind of judgment — who have not allowed the convenience of automated decision-making to entirely displace the slower, harder, more uncertain process of actually deciding what they think is right. This capacity is not preserved automatically. It requires practice, attention, and the willingness to remain present in the gap between what the system says and what you decide to do.

And it requires something else that the Gita names but that modern discourse about AI rarely reaches: the willingness to act from duty even when the outcomes cannot be guaranteed. Every person who maintains evaluative oversight of an AI system — who refuses to let convenience become permission to stop thinking — is practicing a version of what Krishna was describing on the plain of Kurukshetra. They are doing what their role requires, with the skill their nature allows, without the paralysis that comes from demanding a guaranteed result before acting. That is not a small thing. That is precisely the quality of person that this moment needs. The alignment that matters most is not the alignment of systems to goals — it is the alignment of people to what their particular moment and their particular role actually require. Technical alignment follows from that. It does not precede it.

The Gita does not promise that dharmic action produces comfortable outcomes. It promises that it produces the right ones. These are not always the same.

Arjuna fought. The battle was devastating. Many people he loved died. The victory was not clean, not painless, not permanent — history never is. But Arjuna acted according to what his situation required, with the skill his life had prepared him for, and without the paralysis that comes from demanding guarantees before moving.

This is what we are being asked to *do.*

***

DHARMA IN ORDINARY LIFE

The Gita is an extraordinary text, and it is sometimes treated as applicable only to extraordinary situations — moments of civilisational decision, choices that will reshape history. This reading misses what makes it useful. Krishna's instruction to Arjuna was not primarily about the specific choice to fight at Kurukshetra. It was about how to act at all — in any situation, in any role, in any moment where the right course is not clear, and the cost of acting is real, and the option of not acting is itself a choice.

Most of us are not Arjuna. We are not facing choices that will determine the outcome of a war. We are facing choices about what work to take on and how to do it, about what to prioritise and what to let go, about what to build and what to refuse to build, about what to say in meetings and what to push back on, about what our organisations should become and how much of ourselves to invest in making them that. These are not small choices. Collectively, they constitute the texture of the society we are building, and they are made by ordinary people in ordinary moments that feel unmemorable at the time and turn out to matter.

The specific dharma of a software engineer who is asked to build a system that targets users in ways the engineer believes are harmful is not the same as the dharma of an executive who controls the decision to deploy that system. The dharma of a regulator who can create accountability mechanisms is not the same as the dharma of a journalist who can make the absence of those mechanisms visible. The dharma of an educator deciding what to teach children about AI is not the same as that of a parent deciding how much screen time to allow.

But they are all dharma in the original sense: each is an orientation toward what one's specific role and capacity actually requires. Each calls for acting from the position you actually occupy, with the capabilities you actually have, toward the outcomes that your position and capabilities can actually influence. This is not heroic. It is precise. It is the opposite of waiting for someone else to do the large, dramatic thing that will make the small things unnecessary.

The people in this book — Raj, Maya, Ananya, Arjun, Aarav, Rahul, Sara — are practicing versions of this. Not perfectly. Not without confusion and setback. But directionally: they are each, in their specific domain, trying to figure out what the moment actually requires of someone in their position and then acting on that understanding rather than on the more comfortable alternative of waiting for clarity that may never come. Raj rebuilt his practice around judgment rather than analysis because that was what his specific professional position required. Maya maintained her evaluative capacity alongside the diagnostic system because that was what her specific professional role demanded. Sara wrote legislation even though she understood it was inadequate to the full scope of the problem because it was what her specific political role enabled her to do, and doing something adequate was better than waiting to do something comprehensive.

None of them achieved certainty before acting. The Gita does not promise certainty. It promises clarity about what your role requires, and it asks you to act on that clarity rather than waiting for a guarantee of outcome that dharmic action cannot provide and that life, in any era, does not offer.

We are in an era of extraordinary uncertainty about where these technologies are taking us. This uncertainty is real. It is not a reason to be paralysed. It is the normal condition of people in the middle of a transition whose end is not yet visible — people like the first generation that lived with electric grids, or the engineers who had to build railway safety standards before anyone understood how to do it, or the doctors who had to learn what to do with antibiotics before anyone had developed the protocols. They acted out of uncertainty because that was what they had. What they could control was the orientation of their action: toward what sustains, toward what holds together, toward what their specific role actually requires.

***

This is what we are being asked to do.

To act.

From our specific position.

With whatever capacity we have.

In the direction of what holds things together.

That is dharma.

That is what this particular age requires of us.

Not drama.

Not paralysis.

Not the performance of concern without the action that concern demands.

Dharma.

The thing that holds.

PART IV

The Choice

Every generation inherits a world it did not make. Only some decide what kind of world they leave.

CHAPTER 12

The World My Daughter Will Inherit

"We do not inherit the earth from our ancestors. We borrow it from our children."

— Origin uncertain; widely attributed as a Native American proverb

She asked me the question on a Wednesday evening in October, the kind of evening that smells like the end of something — the sky going dark earlier than it had the week before, a coolness in the air that had not been there in summer. Suhana was seven years old. She was sitting on the floor of the living room, half-watching something on a tablet, half-braiding the hair of a doll that had seen better days. The doll had been her favourite for two years and had the slightly battered quality of something that had been genuinely loved.

I was at the dining table, working. Or trying to. I had been staring at the same paragraph for twenty minutes when she looked up and asked, without particular urgency, the way seven-year-olds ask things — as if the question had simply occurred to her and the appropriate response was to say it out loud: "Baba, why does the phone need to know things?"

I put down my pen and asked. "What do you mean?"

"The phone already knows things," she said. She picked up the tablet briefly, then set it back down on the carpet. "It knows what I like to watch. It knows where we live. It knows what Mama likes to eat when we order from the restaurant. Why does it need to know more? Why does it keep asking for more?"

I sat for a moment with the question. Seven-year-olds ask questions with a directness that adults have long since learned to muffle. They have not yet acquired the habit of pre-dismissing their own curiosity. They have not yet internalized the social signal that certain questions, while obviously worth asking, are somehow naive in their simplicity. Suhana had not been taught to accept the architecture of the technology surrounding her without examination. She had simply looked at it and found it puzzling.

She was asking a question that I had spent years studying — that conference rooms full of executives had debated, that philosophers and technologists and regulators had filled volumes trying to answer — and she had arrived at its essential core on her own, from the floor of the living room, in the middle of braiding a doll's hair.

"I'm still finding the answer," I told her.

She nodded, apparently satisfied that this was an honest response, and went back to the doll. Preethi appeared in the doorway from the kitchen, having caught the last exchange. She looked at me without saying anything. After sixteen years together, Preethi and I have entire conversations without speaking a word. What her expression said, standing in that doorway, was something like: that's the right answer. Keep looking.

I sat with Suhana's question for a long time after she went to bed. Not the technical answer — I knew the technical answer, or at least I knew several versions of it. The question she had asked was not technical. It was a question about intent. About appetite. About who benefits from the accumulation, and whether the person being known has any say in how deeply they are known and for what purpose.

It was, in the most precise sense, a question about power. And she was seven.

***

LETTERS WRITTEN INTO THE DARK

During the Second World War, hundreds of thousands of soldiers wrote letters home to children they had not yet met — wives pregnant when they shipped out, babies born during deployments, daughters and sons they knew they might never hold. These letters were not written for history. They were written against the specific terror of the possibility that history would not include the writer. They survive in archives and family collections, are read at anniversaries and memorial services, and are sometimes found in attic boxes long after their writers and first readers are gone.

Reading them is a particular kind of encounter with the past, because they were written not to record what had happened but to reach into a future the writers could not see. The uncertainty in them is palpable — the knowledge that the world their children would inhabit was entirely unknown, that the values and habits the writers held might or might not survive the war, that the specific people they were addressing might grow up in conditions they could not predict.

What is striking about these letters is not the uncertainty. It is the clarity underneath the uncertainty — the clarity about what mattered, arrived at through the proximity of death. Letter after letter describes, with a simplicity made urgent by that proximity, what the writer hoped the world would be. Fairness. Safety. The freedom to choose one's own path. The ability to speak one's mind without fear. The presence of people who keep their promises.

These are not complicated aspirations. They are the things that seem obvious when you are writing to someone who does not yet exist, whose world you cannot control, whose choices you cannot make. They are what you want when you have stripped away everything that is not essential.

There is a letter in the archives of the Imperial War Museum written by a British officer named Leonard who was killed in North Africa in 1943. He had written it to his daughter, who was four months old when he died. She did not read it until she was seventeen. He had written: "I don't know what the world will look like when you read this. I don't know if we will have won. I don't know what will have been built and what will have been lost. But I hope — I hope this with everything in me — that whoever is in charge of things will have remembered that they are in charge of people. That is the only thing I would ask of the future."

Whoever is in charge of things will have remembered that they are in charge of people.

What strikes me about Leonard's letter — about all of these letters, the archives of the articulate grief of parents writing toward children they feared they might not see grow up — is the precision of what they hoped for. Not prosperity, not technological progress, not national power. Safety. Fairness. The freedom to choose. The presence of people who keep their promises. These are relational goods — things that can only exist in the space between people, in the quality of the arrangements that govern how they treat each other.

They are also, it occurs to me, exactly the things that AI systems, well-designed and well-governed, can support. A healthcare system that uses AI to catch diagnoses that would otherwise be missed is one in which more people experience the safety Leonard was writing toward. An educational system that uses AI to give every child access to the depth and quality of instruction once available only to the privileged is one in which more people experience the freedom to choose their own path. A governance system that uses AI to make public services more responsive to the actual needs of the people they serve — rather than the bureaucratic categories that are easiest to administer — is closer to the fairness these letters were written toward.

None of this is guaranteed. The same technologies can be used for surveillance, for manipulation, for the concentration of power in forms that make safety and fairness less available, not more. The technology is not the outcome. The choices made about how to design it, deploy it, govern it, and hold it accountable — those are the outcome. And those choices are being made by people, which means they are subject to all of the wisdom and blindness and self-interest and genuine good faith that human decision-making has always carried.

I read that sentence and thought of Suhana. I thought of the decisions being made right now, in rooms she will never see, by people whose names she does not know, about systems that will be part of the fabric of her world by the time she is old enough to ask who built them and why. I thought about what I would write to her if I were writing into the same dark.

***

WHAT I WOULD TELL HER

I would tell her that she is growing up in the most consequential technological moment in human history. Not because every generation doesn't believe this about its own moment — they do, with some justification — but because this time the evidence is extraordinary. The systems being built now are not faster versions of the tools that came before. They are something qualitatively different: systems that process and synthesise and generate knowledge at a scale and speed that changes what it means for an individual human being to know things, to learn things, to create things. This is not hype. It is the sober assessment of what I have spent two decades watching.

I would tell her this is not something to fear. Fear is appropriate for dangers that can only be escaped. This is something to engage with — with her eyes open, her judgment intact, and her curiosity deployed rather than suppressed.

I would tell her that the people who built these systems were not evil. Most of them were genuinely trying to do something useful, and many succeeded. But they were also — like everyone who has ever built powerful systems — subject to incentives, timelines, competitive pressures, and blind spots that shaped what they built in ways they did not always fully see. She should never mistake the sincerity of the builders for a guarantee of the safety of what was built. These are different things.

I would tell her that the most important skill she can develop — more important than any technical skill, more important than academic achievement of the conventional kind — is the capacity to ask good questions about systems she encounters. Specifically: who designed this, and what did they want to optimise for? Who benefits from how it works, and who bears the costs? What does this system reward, and what does it quietly discourage? What would I lose if this system went away — and would that loss be something I chose to accept?

These are not hostile questions. They are not the questions of someone who distrusts technology. They are the questions of a citizen — someone who has decided that their presence in the world is not passive, who intends to participate in the shaping of the systems that shape them, who refuses the comfortable resignation of "it's too complicated for me to understand."

I would tell her that the future is not something that happens to people. It is something that people *make* — sometimes deliberately, often carelessly, but always through the accumulation of actual choices made by actual human beings in actual moments. She will make choices. They will matter. Not because she is special in some cosmic sense — though she is, to me, in ways I will never adequately express — but because every person who makes choices in the direction of what holds things together is contributing to a world that holds together.

I would tell her about dharma. About dhr — the root that means to hold, to sustain. About Arjuna on the plain of Kurukshetra, unable to act until he was released from the demand for guaranteed outcomes. About the strange freedom that comes from acting from duty rather than from the desire to control results. About what it means to be responsible in a world where the outcomes of your actions extend far beyond what you can see.

I would tell her about hope. Not the hope that things will turn out well — that is not a form of hope that the honest evidence supports unreservedly. But the hope that is distinct from optimism: the decision to act as though things can be better, precisely because that acting is part of what makes them so. The hope that looks clear-eyed at difficulty and continues anyway, not because it is naive but because it understands that the alternative — stopping, withdrawing, concluding that the scale of the problem makes individual engagement irrelevant — is the most reliable way to ensure that things don't improve.

Rebecca Solnit has described hope not as something passive — the lottery ticket clutched on the sofa, the wishful waiting — but as something fundamentally active, something you deploy specifically in emergencies, something closer to a tool you use to break down doors than a feeling you sit with while circumstances unfold. I have thought about that idea many times. It captures something that the comfortable usages of hope often miss: that hope is active, and that it is specifically active in relation to difficult situations, not despite the difficulty but because of it. The difficulty is precisely why you need it.

Suhana will face difficult situations. She will face systems that are more powerful than any individual, organised by interests that are not the same as hers, operated by people who have not thought carefully about whose lives they are shaping. She will face moments when the right action is unclear, the cost of acting is real and the outcome is not guaranteed. These are not unusual situations. They are the ordinary conditions of trying to live responsibly in a complex world. What will matter is what she brings to them.

And I would tell her what I told her when she asked about the phone: I am still finding the answer. But I am looking. And looking is where it starts.

The looking, at least, is happening. In 2021, the World Health Organization published its guidance on the ethics and governance of AI in health — developed through multi-year expert consultation and published by WHO as the authoritative global reference for the field. The document is principled, careful, and illuminating precisely because of what it reveals about the gap between aspiration and mechanism. The six core principles it articulates — protecting autonomy, promoting wellbeing, transparency, accountability, inclusivity, and sustainability — are the right principles. The document is less clear about how they become binding, how violations are identified and addressed, and who has the authority to enforce them. It is, in the language of the previous chapter, a principles document without a constraints document. It describes what good looks like with precision. It is less clear about what prevents bad. That gap — between articulated principle and institutional mechanism — is not a failure of the document. It is the honest description of where the world currently stands. The principles are present. The machinery is still being built. The building is the work.

***

PREETHI

There is a conversation Preethi and I have returned to many times since Suhana asked her question. It is not one conversation — it is many conversations, spread across dinners and weekend mornings and late evenings when the house is quiet and we can say the things we do not say when the day is full. The question underneath all of them is the same: what does it mean to prepare a child for a world you cannot fully predict?

Preethi has thought about this longer and more carefully than I have. She would not say that, but it is true. She sees it from a different angle — not the technology strategist's angle, but the angle of someone who has watched what happens to children when the adults in their lives fail to model the qualities they are supposed to be teaching. She has been watching this for a long time, in ways I am only beginning to properly understand.

"The thing I keep coming back to," she said one evening, "is that we can't give her certainty. The world she's going to inhabit isn't certain. And if we try to give her certainty — if we tell her that things are going to be fine, that the technology will be managed wisely, that the institutions will hold — we're preparing her for a world that doesn't exist. What we can give her is the capacity to navigate uncertainty without being destroyed by it."

"And how do we give her that?" I asked.

"By being honest with her about what we don't know," Preethi said. "By letting her see us navigate uncertainty rather than hiding it from her. By teaching her that not knowing is not the same as being lost — that you can move forward without having all the answers, and that the moving forward is what matters."

We talked for a long time that evening. About what qualities we hoped Suhana would develop. Not skills — skills change too fast to optimise for — but qualities: the capacity for sustained attention in a world engineered for distraction. The ability to hold multiple perspectives simultaneously. The willingness to be wrong and to learn from being wrong. The sense of herself as someone with something to contribute, not merely something to consume.

These are not new qualities. They are old ones — the qualities that every generation of parents has hoped to cultivate in the next, the qualities that good education has always tried to develop, the qualities that are most visible in people whose lives have been well-lived. What is new is the context in which they will be exercised, and the specific forms of pressure they will face.

***

THE WORLD SHE INHERITS

The world Suhana inherits will ask more of her than the world I inherited asked of me. Not because it will be worse — I believe it will be better in many ways. But because its complexity will be greater, its interdependencies more intricate, its systems more powerful and more opaque, their inner workings more recondite and their failure modes less predictable. The gap between what is technically possible and what is genuinely good will be wider, and navigating that gap will require something that cannot be automated: judgment. The kind of judgment that Arjuna needed at Kurukshetra. The kind that is built not by instruction but by practice, by confronting real difficulties in real situations and developing, through that confrontation, the capacity to act rightly under uncertainty.

The single most important investment any parent can make in their child's future is not technical fluency and not academic achievement, though both matter. It is the cultivation of this capacity for judgment: the habit of asking hard questions, the tolerance for ambiguity, the willingness to act without guarantees, and the ethical sensibility that makes judgment not just clever but wise.

The question is not what kind of world she will inherit. The question is what kind of person she will be when she enters it.

***

WHAT PREETHI SAID

I shared a draft of this chapter with Preethi before I shared it with anyone else. She read it twice, which is what she does when she is thinking carefully about something. Then she put it down and looked at me.

"You've written a lot about Suhana's questions," she said. "But not much about how you're answering them. Or not answering them."

This was fair. She was right. I had been writing around something rather than about it: the specific and daily practice of raising a child in a world I do not fully understand, in the presence of technologies I am still learning to evaluate, toward a future I cannot accurately predict.

"I tell her the truth," I said. "I tell her I don't know."

"That's not the same as teaching her what to do when she doesn't know," Preethi said. "That's just not pretending."

Preethi has a way of identifying the gap between what I have said and what I need to say. She has done this for as long as I have known her. It is, I think, one of the more important cognitive functions in our household — the correction of the distance between the idea and the practice of it.

What she was pointing at is real. There is a difference between modelling intellectual humility and actually equipping a child with the tools to navigate uncertainty. Modeling is necessary but not sufficient. Suhana needs, beyond my example of not-knowing, some orientation toward how to not-know productively — how to remain curious rather than anxious, how to ask the next question rather than accept the first answer, how to evaluate a source rather than consume it, how to distinguish what she has been told from what she has actually understood.

These are things that cannot be delivered in a single conversation. They are built over years, in small moments, many of which do not announce themselves as formative. They are built when she brings me a claim she has read online and we sit together and ask where it came from and how we would know if it was right. They are built when she makes a mistake, and we talk about what it reveals rather than treating it as simply an error to move past. They are built when she sees Preethi and me disagree, and we do it openly, and she observes two people who care about getting things right taking the disagreement seriously rather than performing false consensus.

I write this not as a parenting manual — I have more failures in this practice than I care to catalog — but as an acknowledgment of what is actually required. The conversation about technology, about AI, about the future, is not primarily a conversation that happens with policymakers, technologists, and educators. It happens in the small moments of ordinary parenting, in the question that gets taken seriously or dismissed, in the curiosity that gets nurtured or redirected toward something more immediately manageable. The future is built there, in those moments, by all of us, long before it becomes visible as policy or product.

Suhana asked why the phone needs to know things. She is still asking. She will keep asking, in different forms, as the world she inhabits takes shape around her. My job — the job that parenthood gave me before I fully understood what I was taking on — is not to answer that question for her. It is to make sure she keeps asking it. Clearly, persistently, without apology, with whatever tools she develops and whatever wisdom she accumulates.

Her question — why does the phone need to know things? — is the child's version of the civilisational question. We built external memory. We gave it everything. We made it available on demand. The phone needs to know things because we made it the repository of what we have chosen to give it. Suhana will inherit not just the technology but the choices embedded in what it holds and what it was taught to do with what it holds. That inheritance is what this book has been about from the first page.

The world my daughter will inherit is being built right now.

Not by fate.

Not by algorithms.

By choices.

Made by people who could choose differently.

Including me.

Including you.

CHAPTER 13

A Day in the Years Ahead

"You have a right to perform your actions, but never to the fruits of your actions. Let not the fruits of your actions be your motive, nor let your attachment be to inaction."

— *Bhagavad Gita, 2.47*

The early morning light came off the water at a low angle, hitting the glass of the towers at the edge of the Creek, and for a short while before the city fully woke, the streets were cooler and quieter than at any other point in the day. Aarav had grown up here. He still found the morning light surprising.

Aarav had grown up in a world where the externalisation of memory was not an event but a condition — the atmosphere within which everything else happened. He had never known a professional world in which synthesising a decade's worth of research required a decade of human effort. For his generation, external memory was not a disruption. It was infrastructure. The question his generation faced was not whether to use it but how to remain the kind of person who could judge what it produced—and how to avoid becoming, without noticing, a person who had offloaded that judgment along with everything else.

Aarav woke at six-fifteen, not because an alarm told him to but because his body had finally, after years of adolescent resistance, synchronized itself to something resembling a reasonable schedule. He was eighteen now. In six weeks he would begin his first full-time position. This, depending on which version of the conversation he was having, was either a significant milestone or a simple continuation of the work he had been doing in various forms for the past two years.

He lay in the dark for a few minutes with his eyes open, looking at the ceiling — a habit acquired from the period at sixteen when he could not sleep and had learned to use the ceiling as a kind of neutral screen against which to run through whatever he needed to think about before the day began. The ceiling was still there. The habit had outlasted the insomnia.

The question he kept returning to was one his mother had asked him last week, at dinner, with the particular directness she deployed when she had been thinking about something for a while and had finally decided to say it. "Are you happy?" she had asked. "Not about the job. About the life. About the version of things you're moving toward."

He had said yes. He believed he had meant it. But the question had the quality that honest questions from people who love you tend to have: it stayed.

***

MORNING

He got up, pulled on clothes, and went to the kitchen to make tea — a habit acquired from his grandmother, who had lived with them for a year when he was fifteen and who was firmly of the view that the day did not properly begin without it. His grandmother had died the following year, and the tea habit had remained, which was, he had decided, the right kind of inheritance.

The apartment was small — he shared it with two others, both of whom were still asleep at this hour — and the kitchen in the early morning had the particular quality of spaces that belong to no one in particular: the used cups from last night, the half-open window with the city sounds coming through it, the light that was still finding its angle.

He made the tea and stood at the window with it. The street below was beginning to move. The neighbourhood was one of those urban neighbourhoods that had changed significantly in the past decade — not dramatically, not with the kind of obvious disruption that made for clear before-and-after photographs, but with a quality of accumulated change that you noticed mainly when you compared it to what you remembered. Fewer delivery vans clogging the morning street — the logistics had reorganised, and most deliveries now moved through a network of smaller, more efficient systems that operated primarily at night and through pedestrian-scale infrastructure.

More of the street-level space occupied by things that required physical presence: a bakery, a repair café, a community workshop where you could use equipment by the hour, a small health clinic with a walk-in service that had opened two years ago and immediately had a six-week wait.

The neighbourhood felt, in some way he found difficult to articulate, more local than it had when he was a child. More oriented toward what was actually here, rather than toward the delivery of things from elsewhere. He was not sure whether this was a good change or simply a different arrangement of advantages and disadvantages. But it was visible, and he noticed it.

His phone showed him a morning summary — not pushed at him, but available when he picked it up and asked for it. Weather, a note about a meeting at eleven, a message from his colleague Priya about a dataset she had been working on overnight. He read the Priya message carefully, set a reminder to respond before the meeting, and put the phone back on the counter.

He had developed, over the past two years, a deliberate practice around the phone: he consulted it rather than let it consult him. He had noticed, at sixteen, that the direction of attention mattered — that there was a difference between picking up a tool to accomplish something and being summoned by a tool that had decided, through its own logic, that now was a moment he should pay attention to. He had made choices, sometimes awkward ones, about which direction he wanted the attention to flow. The practice was imperfect. It was also, he had concluded, worth the imperfection.

***

THE COMMUTE

He took the metro. The line he used had been partially automated for six years, which meant the trains ran more frequently and more reliably than before, and that the drivers who used to operate them had been retrained into a combination of network management and passenger assistance roles. He knew this because his uncle had been one of those drivers, and his uncle's experience of the transition — complicated, not uniformly positive, ultimately workable — had given him a more concrete understanding of what "workforce transition" actually meant for an actual person than most of the policy papers he had read on the subject.

He found a seat and watched the city through the windows as the train moved. It was the kind of city watching that you can only do when you are in transit and have no obligation to do anything except move from one place to another. The platforms they passed through showed the ordinary morning mix of people heading to work, school, or wherever they were going. A woman reading a physical book. A man having an animated conversation with someone through earbuds. A group of secondary school students with the specific energy of people who have been awake for fewer hours than is ideal. Two workers in high-visibility vests eating something from paper bags.

What the city looked like, he thought, was mostly like a city. The changes were real, but they were distributed through the ordinary fabric of things rather than concentrated in obvious spectacles. The automated logistics systems were there, but they were not dramatic — they were simply how things moved now. The AI-assisted systems in workplaces were there, but for most people most of the time they were simply the tools they used. The governance debates about those systems — which were real, and ongoing, and often contentious — happened in rooms that looked like other rooms where people were trying to figure out complicated problems.

The future, he had concluded, did not look like science fiction. It looked like the present, but reorganised in ways that mattered.

***

WORK: THE DATASET

His position was at an organisation that worked at the intersection of data analysis and civic advocacy — specifically on the question of how algorithmic decision systems were affecting housing access in cities. It was not the most obvious career path for someone who had been primarily interested in climate data at sixteen. But the thread connecting them was visible, if you looked: both were about the gap between what numbers said and what they meant for actual people.

Dr. Farouk — his manager, a woman who had been doing this work for twelve years and who expressed her standards through the quality of her questions rather than the directness of her corrections — had given him his first substantive assignment two weeks before he officially started, because she had learned that the best way to understand whether someone could do the work was to give them some of it and observe what they noticed.

What she had given him was a dataset of housing application outcomes across three districts, over five years, correlated with demographic and economic variables. The algorithmic system that had processed the applications during that period used a risk assessment model to prioritise cases. His task was to evaluate whether the model's outputs had been equitable across different demographic groups.

He had spent two weeks with the data. What he found was not a smoking gun. Nothing pointing to deliberate bias. Nothing that would produce a clean headline. What he found was something more ambiguous and, in some ways, more troubling: a systematic pattern in which applicants from certain postal codes, regardless of their individual financial profiles, received lower priority scores. And those postal codes correlated — not perfectly, not exclusively, but significantly — with historically underserved communities.

The model had not been designed to penalise anyone. The designers had, by all accounts, tried to build something fair. They had even tested it for specific types of bias before deployment. But the model had been trained on historical data. And historical data contained the residue of historical decisions — about which neighbourhoods received investment, which communities had access to stable employment, which families had been able to build the credit histories that the model's training data treated as proxies for risk.

The model had learned, faithfully and efficiently, from the past. It had automated the past. And the past, in housing in this city, as in most cities, contained decades of decisions that had not been fair.

***

WORK: THE MEETING

At eleven o'clock he joined Dr. Farouk's team meeting — seven people around a table in the organisation's small conference room, the walls covered in printed maps of the districts they worked in, handwritten annotations marking the neighbourhoods they were currently analyzing. There was something Aarav had noticed about this organisation's physical space: it was full of printed things. Maps, charts, excerpts from reports, photographs of the communities they worked with. In an era when almost everything could be digital and virtual, the people in this room had made a deliberate choice to keep some of it physical.

He had asked Dr. Farouk about this once. She had thought about it for a moment. "When it's on the wall," she said, "you can't close the tab. You have to keep looking at it. That matters for this kind of work." He had written that down.

The meeting began with a review of his dataset analysis. He walked through the findings — the postal code correlation, the historical data problem, the specific pattern in the priority scoring. He was careful to be accurate about what the data showed and what it did not show. He had spent a significant portion of his two weeks on this precision because he had learned, from watching people work with data, that the most persuasive misuse of evidence was one that slightly overreached what the data actually demonstrated.

When he finished, the room was quiet for a moment.

"What you've found," Dr. Farouk said, "is a discrimination problem, but it's not located where discrimination problems are usually imagined to be located. It's not in the algorithm itself, in the sense of the algorithm containing an explicit rule that treats groups differently. It's in the training data. And that's harder to fix, and harder to explain to a regulatory body, and harder to attribute responsibility for, because it happened before the algorithm was built."

"Whose responsibility is it?" Aarav asked.

"That's exactly the right question," she said. "And the answer is genuinely contested. The designers who built the model? The city agency that provided the training data? The policymakers who created the conditions that led to the historical data looking the way it does? All of them? None of them exclusively?" She paused. "We're going to present this to the housing authority next month. They'll ask the same question. You should have an answer that's useful rather than just accurate."

He spent the rest of the morning revising his analysis with that framing in mind — trying to distinguish between what the data showed, what it meant, and what it implied for action. These were three different things, and collapsing them, he was learning, was one of the most reliable ways to produce analysis that was technically correct and practically useless.

***

LUNCH: THE NEIGHBORHOOD

At noon, he walked to the district where his data had been collected. He had decided, two days into the assignment, that he needed to see it. Not because the data were insufficient — they were comprehensive. But because the data was about specific streets and specific buildings and specific people who had been affected by the scoring patterns he had documented, and he found that keeping that specificity in mind — the physical reality of the place rather than its statistical representation — changed how he thought about the work.

The neighbourhood was ordinary in the way that most neighbourhoods are ordinary when you are in them rather than looking at them from a data set. The streets were not dramatic.

There was a fruit market, a school with children visible through the fence during what appeared to be a break, a hardware store, a laundromat. The buildings were a mix of ages — some clearly old, others newer construction from the past decade, in a style that was efficient but not especially beautiful.

What you could see, if you looked for it, was the accumulation of the housing policy decisions that his dataset had documented. Buildings where maintenance had been deferred for years. Families in units that were technically adequate and practically overcrowded. A community centre that the neighbourhood association had fundraised to build, that was clearly well-used, and that sat across the street from a building whose ground-floor unit had been empty for three years because the landlord was holding it for a commercial tenant who never came.

He ate lunch at a small café near the community centre and watched the neighbourhood move around him. The data he had analysed was about these streets, these buildings, these people who were going about their Wednesday with the ordinary purposefulness of people who have things to do. The algorithm that had produced the priority scoring patterns he had found had never been to this street. It had never seen the community centre or the overdue maintenance or the empty ground floor unit. It had seen a postal code, correlated with historical data, and produced a number.

He thought about what Dr. Farouk had said: a useful answer rather than just an accurate one. What would be useful here was not a more accurate algorithm. It was a housing authority that understood what its algorithm could not see.

***

THE REPORT, REVISED

He returned to the office and spent the afternoon revising his report for the third time. The first version had been the technical analysis — accurate, thorough, written for a reader who understood data science. The second version incorporated Dr. Farouk's feedback on distinguishing what the data showed from what they meant. The third version was the hardest: trying to write for a housing authority that would include people who were defensive about the system they had built, people who were genuinely worried about their constituents, and people who were primarily concerned about legal liability.

He had learned something about audiences from his two years of working with data: the facts of a situation and the persuasiveness of those facts to a specific audience were almost entirely separate problems. Data was not self-interpreting. Even the most unimpeachable finding required translation into a frame that a specific set of people, with their specific concerns and their specific institutional interests, could actually receive. A perfectly accurate analysis could be completely unpersuasive to the audience it was meant to reach, because accuracy and persuasiveness operated according to different logics. This did not mean distorting the facts. It meant understanding what the audience already believed, what they were afraid of, what they were trying to protect, and framing the accurate information in a way that engaged with those specifics rather than ignoring them.

He sent the revised report to Dr. Farouk at five-thirty. She responded within twenty minutes: "This is significantly better. One more thing — add a section on what good would look like. Not just what the problem is. What the housing authority could do specifically that would address it? They need something to move toward, not just something to move away from." He made a note and closed his laptop.

***

EVENING

He met Dhruv for dinner at a restaurant near the metro station. This place had opened two years ago and that they had been going to with enough regularity that the owner, a middle-aged man named Shiv who seemed constitutionally incapable of letting anyone eat without telling them something interesting about the food, had started to recognise them.

Shiv brought their usual drinks without being asked and told them that the tomatoes for the evening's dal had come from a cooperative farm thirty kilometers from the city that had switched to a community-supported agriculture model three years ago and was now supplying twelve restaurants in the neighbourhood. "You're eating something that was grown by a specific person on a specific plot of land," he said. "I think that matters. I don't know if it matters in any way I can measure. But I think it does." He went back to the kitchen.

Dhruv watched him go. "He says that every time," he said.

"I know," Aarav said. "I think he means it every time."

They talked about their days. Dhruv was apprenticed to an architecture practice that worked primarily on adaptive reuse — converting buildings that had been designed for one purpose into buildings that served a different one. The practice had more work than it could handle, because the past decade had left a landscape of commercial real estate that no longer served its original function and had to be reimagined into something else. Dhruv found the work interesting, which Aarav had concluded was the most reliable indicator of a good professional choice.

Eventually the conversation found its way to where it usually went when they were being honest with each other.

"Are you scared?" Dhruv asked. Not about anything specific. The general question — about the world they were entering, and what it was becoming, and whether there would be a place in it that felt like theirs.

Aarav thought about it properly before answering. "Not scared," he said. "More like — aware. Alert. Like I know the terrain is complicated and I want to navigate it carefully rather than confidently."

"What's the difference?"

"Confidence assumes you know where you're going," Aarav said. "Careful assumes you don't, and that knowing you don't is an advantage rather than a weakness."

Dhruv nodded slowly. "My grandmother says something like that. She says her generation confused confidence with competence for about forty years and it cost them." He paused. "She's eighty-three. She's still right about most things. It's inconvenient."

Aarav laughed. The laughter felt uncomplicated, unlike many others. They ordered food and talked about other things — about Dhruv's building project, about a film they had both watched and disagreed about, about the restaurant Shiv was apparently planning to open a second location of, on a street two neighbourhoods over. The city moved around them, full of people making small decisions that would add up to something nobody had fully planned.

***

NIGHT

Walking home through the evening streets, Aarav thought about his mother's question: are you happy? Not about the job.

About the life. About the version of things you're moving toward.

He thought about the dataset he had spent two weeks with, and the neighbourhood he had walked through at lunch, and the housing authority presentation he was going to help prepare. He thought about the report revision Dr. Farouk had asked him to do — the section on what good would look like. He had been thinking about that section since she asked for it, and he was beginning to have a sense of what it should say.

He thought about his mother at her kitchen table that morning, with her tea and her tablet and her seventeen years of watching students navigate the difference between information and understanding. He thought about what she had said: the things that mattered most about teaching — seeing a student suddenly understand something they couldn't see before — those were still there. She had protected them by remembering that they were the point.

He did not know yet what the enterprise of his life was actually for. He was eighteen. He had time to find out. But he was paying attention — to the data and to what the data could not capture, to the numbers and to the people the numbers were supposed to represent, to the systems he worked inside and to the questions those systems could not answer.

That, at least, seemed like a start. And he was beginning to think that starting well, carefully, with genuine attention to what was actually happening, was not a modest thing. It was most of what the moment required.

At his kitchen table, with the tea steeping for exactly four minutes in the habit he had learned from his grandmother and had never quite been able to explain to people who asked why he was so particular about it, he opened his laptop and started writing.

He wrote: "What good would look like is a housing system that uses predictive analysis to identify need, not to determine outcome. That uses the algorithm to prioritise attention, not to automate decision. That pairs every algorithmic output with a human who knows the neighbourhood and has authority to override the output when what they see on the street contradicts what the data shows. That tracks not just the decisions the system makes but the decisions humans make when they override it, and learns from both."

He paused and looked at what he had written. It was, he thought, too abstract. He had spent a week with data about a specific neighbourhood, and he had walked those streets at noon, and he had seen the community centre and the empty ground-floor unit and the overdue maintenance that no algorithm had flagged because algorithms saw patterns in data and not the specific faces of the people who lived with the consequences of those patterns.

He revised: "What good would look like is a housing authority that on every sixth morning sends a team of two people — one who understands the data and one who knows the community — to walk a different block in the priority dataset. Not to inspect. Not to assess. To see. To be the corrective that the algorithm cannot provide for itself: the human presence that notices what the numbers cannot."

He wrote and revised for an hour. Outside, the city had quieted to its late-night register: the occasional vehicle, the sound of someone's window opening and closing two floors up, the distant horn of a train on the elevated line. He sent the revised section to Dr. Farouk with a brief note: "The addition you asked for. I walked the neighbourhood today. I think it changed what I thought the recommendation should be."

He closed the laptop and sat for a moment with the tea he had forgotten to drink, which had gone cold. The window was slightly open. The air coming through it smelled of the city — asphalt and jasmine from someone's balcony garden and the faint presence of rain that had not yet arrived.

He thought: the future is being built by people who are deciding, right now, what their systems are for. The good news is that they are people. The challenge is that they are also — like him, like everyone — people who see what they see and miss what they miss, who are shaped by what they have been taught and limited by what they have not been taught, who bring their specific histories to the specific decisions in front of them. The work is to see more, to know more, and to stay humble enough about what you are still missing to keep looking.

The future does not arrive.

It accumulates.

One decision at a time,

made by people who were paying attention

and people who were not.

Aarav went to sleep.

In the morning he would read Dr. Farouk's reply.

She would say: yes.

Exactly this.

Add it to the report.

CHAPTER 14

Alignment Is the Only Scalable Power

"In every deliberation, we must consider the impact on the seventh generation, even if it requires having skin as thick as the bark of a pine."

— Great Law of the Haudenosaunee (Iroquois Confederacy)

Somewhere between twelve and twenty-five generations ago, the historians disagree sharply on the date, with estimates ranging from the twelfth century to around 1600 CE, and ongoing scholarship placing the most likely founding around 1450 CE, a council of leaders from five nations in the northeastern woodlands of what is now North America came together to form what they called the Haudenosaunee Confederacy: the Great League of Peace. In English, it is often called the Iroquois Confederacy. The people themselves have always used the name they gave it.

The confederacy created a constitution, one of the most sophisticated governance documents in pre-modern history, passed down through generations by memory and wampum record before being set down in text in the nineteenth century. At the centre of this constitution was a principle considered foundational to all legitimate decision-making:

In every deliberation, we must consider the impact on the seventh generation.

Seven generations, at an average of 25 years per generation, is approximately 175 years. The governing councils were not asked to predict the future with precision, no one can do that. They were asked to hold it in mind. To let the weight of those unborn descendants press on every decision, so that the easy choice and the right choice could never be entirely separated.

What strikes me about this principle, reading it now, is not its ambition. It is its humility. The principle does not claim to know what the seventh generation will want or need. It acknowledges that this is unknowable. It simply says: let that unknowability make you careful. Let the existence of people you will never meet inform the seriousness with which you take your choices today.

The Haudenosaunee Confederacy lasted for centuries. It influenced, directly and indirectly, the constitutional thinking of some of the American founders, Benjamin Franklin studied it carefully and held it up as an example of successful multinational governance. It is, by any measure, one of the great experiments in durable political organisation that human history has produced.

It was built by people who thought about the seventh generation.

We are now being asked to think about ours.

***

ARJUN, SEVERAL YEARS LATER

I had been thinking about Arjun Sharma, the financial analyst who sat in his car in the parking garage for twenty minutes after a client meeting, unable to explain clearly what he did for a living, when I ran into the second chapter of his story.

Not Arjun himself. A version of his trajectory: the person who had been expert at something that was now being done differently, who had been required to figure out what, if anything, they still had to offer in the new configuration.

The versions of this story that end badly are the ones I hear most, because they are more dramatic. The versions that end well are quieter, and they tend to share a particular quality: the person did not waste time trying to convince themselves that the change was not real, or that their existing expertise would somehow be sufficient without adaptation, or that the right response was to resist and wait. They asked a different question instead. Not "how do I preserve what I was?" but "what, in the new situation, actually needs me?"

Arjun, in the version of events I was told, eventually found his footing in the work of what some people in his field were calling orchestration — not building the systems, not running the systems, but understanding them well enough to know when they were right, when they were wrong, when they were right for the wrong reasons, and when to override them in the specific, consequential situations where human judgment remained not just valuable but irreplaceable. He had spent six months thinking he had no viable future in finance. He spent the following years becoming genuinely indispensable in ways he had not previously been, because the scarcity that mattered had shifted from "who can analyse the data?" to "who can tell me what the analysis means for this specific decision, with this specific risk profile, at this specific moment?"

The difference, as he described it to a colleague who described it to me, was not primarily technical. It was about deciding what kind of actor he wanted to be in a changed world. Not a victim of the change. Not a denier of it. A navigator, someone who understood the new terrain well enough to move through it with intention rather than confusion.

***

RAJ, THREE YEARS LATER

And Raj, the consultant who had stared at a forty-seven-second analysis on a Tuesday morning with a cup of pod coffee going cold, had spent three years arriving at a clarity he had not expected to feel the way he did.

It had taken three years because the distance he had to travel was different from Arjun's. Arjun had had to find a new role within his existing field. Raj had had to rethink what his field was for, what the fundamental value of strategy consulting was in a world where the research and synthesis layer had become relatively cheap and fast. What he had arrived at, through difficult client conversations and honest self-assessment, was this: the value of a good strategy advisor lay primarily not in the analysis. It was in the interpretation, the capacity to understand what a finding meant for a specific organisation, with its specific history and culture and stakeholder dynamics, and to help that organisation navigate from understanding to action.

He had a meeting, about eight months into that reckoning, that he has described to me as the one that clarified everything. A financial services firm, a major restructuring decision, a lot of money in the balance. Raj had spent two weeks building the context that the AI systems could not build: the internal political dynamics, the two executives whose rivalry was shaping the options, the regulatory history that made certain pathways more viable than they appeared on paper. He arrived at the meeting with a recommendation that was, he believed, correct, and more importantly, that was correct in the specific way that only someone who understood this particular organisation could know.

The client had already decided, not in the room, before he arrived. They had run the numbers through a faster, cheaper system the week before, and the outputs had pointed the same direction, and the board had signed off. They were professional and courteous about it. They thanked him for the additional context. They said it was useful background.

He drove home. He had been right. It had not mattered this time. The judgment he had brought, the specific, contextual, irreplaceable human read of a situation, had arrived after the decision had already been made by a system that was cheaper and faster and had delivered a sufficient answer to the people who needed to move on.

He had expected to feel diminished. He did not. He felt something closer to clarity. "The analysis was always a means," he said, in a conversation I have returned to many times. "The judgment was always the thing. I was right. They moved anyway. That is also the world. Acting from what you actually know, and releasing the outcome — I had been reading the Gita for years, and I had not understood what that meant until that drive home."

***

WHAT ALIGNMENT ACTUALLY MEANS

The word "alignment" has entered the mainstream conversation about AI primarily as a technical term, the challenge of ensuring that AI systems pursue goals beneficial to humans rather than proxy objectives that diverge in harmful ways. This is an important technical challenge, and serious researchers are working on it with genuine urgency. There are real problems in this space that require solutions that do not yet exist.

But alignment, understood more broadly, is not just a property of systems. It is a property of choices — of the orientations that individuals, organisations, and institutions bring to the decisions they make about what to build, how to deploy it, and what accountability structures to maintain around it.

The most important alignment question is not whether the systems can be made to pursue good goals. It is whether the people and institutions deploying those systems can be organised around good goals — whether the incentives, accountability structures, governance mechanisms, and cultural norms can be brought into sufficient coherence with genuine human wellbeing that the technology serves rather than distorts.

This is a harder problem than the technical one. Not because human beings are irredeemably corrupt, but because the systems that shape human behaviour — markets, institutions, incentive structures, cultural expectations — have their own momentum, their own embedded logic, their own tendency to optimise for what is measurable at the expense of what is merely important. Aligning those systems with long-term human flourishing has been the central challenge of governance for as long as there has been governance. Every generation has had to take it up again, in the specific form that their particular moment required.

The Haudenosaunee had a practice for this. They slowed down. They held the seventh generation in mind. They made the weight of the future a present constraint on decision-making rather than a future problem to be dealt with later. They institutionalised the long view — embedded it in the structure of their governance so that it was not optional, not dependent on the wisdom of any individual leader, but required by the system itself.

We have not yet found our equivalent practice for the decisions we are making about AI. But finding it is not optional. It is the work.

***

WHAT THIS REQUIRES OF YOU

Five orientations. Not rules — these cannot be rules, because the situations that require them are too various and too fast-moving to be captured in rules. They are dispositions: ways of approaching a world in which human judgment and machine capability will have to work together for the foreseeable future, neither fully trusting the other nor fully able to do without it. They compound. A person or organisation that develops all five is not just individually positioned better — they are contributing to the cultural shift that makes governance possible at all.

DISCERNMENT

Every system — technological, organisational, cultural — rewards some behaviours and discourages others. The algorithm that determines which content you see rewards specific emotional responses. The performance review rewards specific kinds of contribution and makes others invisible. The hiring system was optimised for specific signals and was blind to others. Ask what each system you participate in actually rewards — not what it claims to reward. The gap between the two is where the unintended consequences live.

Discernment is the capacity to ask that question persistently, and to teach others to ask it. If you teach, if you parent, if you mentor — the most enduring thing you can offer is not competence in a specific domain. Competence becomes obsolete on timescales now measurable in years. Discernment — the habit of asking: what is this for? Who designed this? What could go wrong? What am I not seeing? — compounds across contexts and over time. NYC Local Law 144, which in 2023 became the first legislation requiring mandatory independent bias audits of AI hiring tools, was passed because enough people in the room kept asking those questions until they became policy. Discernment aggregates.

DEPENDENCY

Every tool creates dependency. This is not a problem to be solved — it is a condition to be understood. The relevant question is not whether you depend on a system but whether you know what you depend on, and what happens when it fails or behaves unexpectedly. The physician who knows what the diagnostic system is good at and what it is likely to miss is in a fundamentally different position from the physician who simply accepts its outputs. Both are dependent. Only one understands the dependency.

Develop the habit of asking: if this system were unavailable tomorrow, what would I be unable to do? The answer to that question is important information about where your own capabilities need to remain sharp. The organisations that navigate technological transitions well are those that maintain enough internal expertise to evaluate their own tools — not just their outputs, but their reasoning, assumptions, and failure modes. This is expensive. It is less expensive than discovering a systematic error three years in because nobody retained enough knowledge to notice it.

DELIBERATION

Speed is not always an advantage. For decisions that are complex, high-stakes, or irreversible, deliberation is not a cost — it is the mechanism by which errors are identified before they compound into consequences that cannot be undone. The pressure to move fast is often appropriate and sometimes necessary. It is also one of the ways accountability gets lost — when there is no time to ask who will be affected, and how, and whether there is a better option. Protect the spaces in your professional and personal life that allow for slow thinking. They are rarer than they should be and more valuable than they appear.

There is also a strong temptation, when systems become large and complex and opaque, to disengage from governing them — to conclude that the decisions are being made by people with more power or more technical knowledge, and that your own participation is therefore irrelevant. This conclusion is almost always wrong, and self-fulfilling: the more people disengage, the more governance becomes the exclusive province of those with the greatest interest in shaping it to their advantage. Stay in the room. Ask questions—express preferences. Refuse the resignation that masquerades as sophistication.

DEPTH

The information environment created by AI systems creates a particular pressure toward breadth — toward knowing a little about many things, toward the kind of synthesised summary awareness that feels comprehensive but lacks the texture of genuine understanding. This pressure is real and, in modest doses, not harmful. It becomes a problem when it substitutes for depth — when the summary replaces the source, when the overview substitutes for the detailed knowledge that would reveal its oversimplifications.

Depth compounds in ways that breadth does not. A deep understanding of a specific domain — the history of a particular technology, the details of a specific regulatory framework, the accumulated experience of working in a specific context over many years — produces insights and recognitions that no surface-level synthesis can replicate. It also generates the most useful questions to ask of AI systems, because the deep expert knows what the system is likely to have gotten wrong and which important nuances a summary would naturally flatten. Invest in going deep somewhere, even if the incentive structures of your environment consistently push toward breadth.

TRUST

Every relationship — between people, between institutions, between institutions and the people they serve — runs on a reserve of trust that accumulates slowly and depletes quickly. Trust cannot be manufactured at the moment it is needed. It can only be drawn on. Build it now, in the ordinary moments that do not seem to matter, because when the moments that do matter arrive, the reserve you have built is all you will have to draw on.

Every act of epistemic cowardice — the avoided question, the convenient imprecision, the gap between stated principle and actual practice — is a small borrowing against future credibility. Coherence compounds. An organisation that builds genuine accountability structures — where commitments are monitored, where failures are acknowledged and investigated rather than managed, where the gap between what is claimed and what is done is treated as important information — builds trust that makes every future difficulty easier to navigate. An organisation that performs accountability builds nothing. The crisis, when it comes, finds an empty reserve.

***

THE RIVER

I want to end where I began — with the question of memory.

The systems we have built are, at their most profound, a form of external memory — repositories of the accumulated output of human civilisation, made queryable in ways that are unprecedented. This is what the title of this book means: LLM as Life Long Memories. Not metaphor. Description.

But before I reach the end of this argument, I want to linger for a moment on what the argument asks of each of us — not as a civilisation, but as individuals, in the specific contexts we actually inhabit.

The case I have made is about civilisational scale: about the concentration of power in AI infrastructure, about the governance of systems that affect hundreds of millions of people, about the long-run consequences of choices being made right now in corporate boardrooms and government ministries and academic research programmes. These are real and urgent concerns. They are also, for most people, concerns about systems they have limited direct influence over.

What most people have direct influence over is smaller, and it matters. It matters because the large-scale outcomes are built from the accumulation of small-scale choices — about what we build, what we use, how we use it, what we resist, what we insist on, what we teach our children, what we tolerate in our institutions, what we require of our leaders. These choices, made individually, aggregate into the conditions that make the large-scale choices either more or less possible.

A person who has developed the habit of asking what a system rewards does not simply think more clearly about their own choices. They become, in their professional context, someone who models that habit for others — who demonstrates that the question is askable, who surfaces implications that others had not articulated, who makes it slightly more likely that the organisation they inhabit makes choices with awareness rather than purely with automation. The individual practice becomes, slowly, through accumulated influence, organisational culture. Organisational culture becomes, slowly, through accumulated example, sector-wide norm. Sector-wide norm becomes, over time, the invisible infrastructure of expectation within which regulation eventually becomes possible.

This is a slow process. It is not the only process needed — legislative action and corporate accountability are also needed, and are more direct. But it is the process that operates at the level where most of us actually live, and dismissing it as insufficiently impactful is a way of avoiding the responsibility that actually falls to us.

None of the people in this book — Raj, Maya, Ananya, Arjun, Aarav, Rahul, Sara — changed the world by themselves. They changed the small patch of it that they occupied, through the accumulation of choices made with more awareness than the average, through the insistence on asking questions that would have been easier not to ask, through the refusal to entirely outsource their judgment to systems whose workings they did not fully understand. The world, if it improves, will improve through the aggregate of those choices made by ordinary people in ordinary contexts who chose to be slightly more present, slightly more questioning, slightly more responsible than they were otherwise incentivised to be.

Memory matters because it is the basis of all learning. You cannot improve without it. You cannot identify patterns, course-correct, or build on what came before without the capacity to carry the past into the present. The civilisation that learns from its history is the civilisation capable of building a future different from it.

But memory alone is not enough. What gives memory its value is the judgment with which it is interpreted and applied. A person who remembers everything but understands nothing is not wiser than someone who has forgotten most things but learned from what they experienced. The same is true at civilisational scale. The accumulation of information is not the same as the accumulation of wisdom. The Library of Alexandria burned, and civilisation mourned it. But civilisation also continued — because the books were not the civilisation. The people who had learned from the books were the civilisation. What mattered was what they had internalized, what they had made part of their practice, what they carried forward when the building was gone.

What we need — what this moment asks for — is the capacity to hold both: the external memory that our systems now make available, and the wisdom that remains irreducibly human. Not in opposition to each other, but in genuine collaboration. The capability and the constraint that gives it direction. The river and its banks.

***

WHAT COHERENCE ACTUALLY COMPOUNDS

The phrase I used earlier — "coherence compounds" — is worth examining directly, because it is easy to read as vague optimism, and I mean it more precisely.

Incoherence, in systems and in organisations and in cultures, operates like debt: it accumulates interest. Every act of epistemic cowardice — the avoided question, the convenient imprecision, the gap between stated principle and actual practice — is a small borrowing against future credibility. Every decision made without understanding its implications for other decisions creates a small incoherence. Every commitment that cannot be kept creates a small erosion of trust. Every process that optimises for a measurable proxy at the expense of an important but unmeasurable outcome creates a small misalignment. These accumulate. Over time, they compound — not in the way that financial interest compounds, smoothly and predictably, but in the way that institutional problems compound: slowly and then suddenly, as small misalignments interact with each other and with external pressures to produce crises that appear dramatic but have been building for years.

Coherence works in the opposite direction. An organisation that builds genuine accountability structures — where commitments are monitored, where failures are acknowledged and investigated rather than managed, where the gap between what is claimed and what is done is treated as important information rather than a communications problem — creates a different kind of compound effect. It builds trust, which reduces the friction of every future interaction. It builds a culture in which problems surface before they compound, which reduces the cost of addressing them. It builds a reputation that attracts the kind of people and clients and partners who want to work with organisations that take their commitments seriously.

This is why I say coherence is the only power that scales. Raw capability — the ability to do things — is more fungible than it appears. A sufficiently capable actor without coherence eventually produces outcomes that undermine their own interests, because the incoherence accumulates until it breaks something. A less capable actor with genuine coherence builds something that compounds in ways that capability alone cannot. This is as true for AI systems as it is for the organisations that build them: a system of extraordinary capability deployed without the institutional coherence to govern it well will eventually produce consequences that its builders will not have anticipated and that the people affected by it will not have consented to.

The institutions, practices, and governance structures that we are trying to build around AI capability are the banks. They are not trying to stop the river. They are trying to ensure that its power flows in directions that are livable for the people whose land it runs through.

Coherence compounds. A system that moves in the right direction, consistently, over a long enough time, arrives somewhere worth arriving. That is the only kind of power that scales.

We did not build artificial intelligence. We built civilisation's external memory. That distinction — which sounds philosophical but is, in practice, entirely concrete — runs through every chapter of this book and will run through every decade of the century ahead. How you relate to the external memory your civilisation has built, in your specific role, with your specific capacity, in the specific moment you actually inhabit, is the question the book has been building toward. Five orientations follow. They are not answers. They are the practices that make answering possible.

Rahul worked on contract assignments for the 18 months after the restructuring. Three contracts in that time — the work was available, but it was not the same work, and it did not pay the same, and it did not feel the same. He was not broken. He was managing. He had not pivoted. He had adjusted, downward, to what was available, not yet knowing that the work he would eventually find — the smaller organisation, the quality audit, the slow task of making AI infrastructure intelligible to the people who depended on it — was already forming somewhere ahead of him, though he could not see it from eighteen months out.

The books we write, including this one, tend to find the people we follow after they have found their shape. Rahul's three years between goodbye drinks and that smaller organisation were not clean. Eighteen months looked one way. Three years looked different. The in-between — the contract work, the downward adjustment, the slow accumulation of what eventually becomes the new footing — is the part that narrative tends to elide. It is worth naming. It is where most people actually live, for longer than the story usually shows.

The Gita does not promise that acting from dharma produces good outcomes. It promises the right action. Rahul's displacement was not a failure of dharma. It was the cost this transition is asking certain people to bear — not because they deserve it, but because of where they happened to be standing when the ground shifted.

Suhana asked why the phone needs to know things. She was seven. The answer this book has been building toward is not that the phone doesn't need to know — it does, and it will, and that is not the question worth asking anymore. The question worth asking is what we want it to remember about us. It does remember. That is the point. And so we must choose — carefully, continuously, from whatever position we hold — what we give it to hold.

These are the same questions, asked across vastly different contexts and across thousands of years. What do we owe to those who come after us? How do we act well when the results are uncertain? What is this system for, and does it serve the people it claims to serve?

These questions have no final answer. They are not the kind of questions that get resolved. They are the kind that have to be asked again and again, in each new context, by each new generation — including the one that is just now becoming old enough to ask them.

Memory without wisdom is storage.

Wisdom without memory is guesswork.

Together, they are the only foundation worth building on.

This is the choice.

This has always been the choice.

The tools are new.

The choice is ancient.

And it is, as it has always been,

ours to make.

Notes on Sources

This book draws on a wide range of historical, scientific, and philosophical sources. What follows is a selective guide to the primary sources and key texts behind each chapter's central arguments and historical narratives, offered for readers who wish to explore further.

Preface & Prologue

The history of the Library of Alexandria is reconstructed from Lionel Casson's Libraries in the Ancient World (Yale University Press, 2001) and Mostafa El-Abbadi's Life and Fate of the Ancient Library of Alexandria (UNESCO, 1990). Mark Weiser's foundational essay "The Computer for the 21st Century" appeared in Scientific American in September 1991 and remains one of the most prescient technology papers of the twentieth century.

Chapter 1 — The Day Time Collapsed

The history of the telegraph and Samuel Morse's demonstration is drawn from Tom Standage's The Victorian Internet (Walker & Company, 1998), which remains the most readable account of the telegraph's social and commercial consequences. Marshall McLuhan's central argument about media as extensions of human faculties appears throughout Understanding Media: The Extensions of Man (McGraw-Hill, 1964). The GitHub Copilot data on developer productivity and security vulnerability rates is drawn from Microsoft Research publications (2023) and reporting in the Proceedings of the IEEE International Symposium on Empirical Software Engineering and Measurement; specifics vary by study and cohort, and readers should consult the primary literature for current findings.

Chapter 2 — Memory Became External

Plato's Phaedrus, in which Socrates tells the story of Thoth and Thamus, is in the public domain (written c. 370 BC). The passage quoted in Chapter 2 draws on the phrasing of Benjamin Jowett's public domain translation (Oxford, 1892), which remains widely cited. Walter Hamilton's Penguin Classics edition (1973) is also accessible and reliable for further reading. Andy Clark's "extended mind" thesis is developed in Being There: Putting Brain, Body, and World Together Again (MIT Press, 1997) and, with David Chalmers, in the paper "The Extended Mind" (Analysis, 1998). The IBM Watson at MD Anderson Cancer Center project is documented in reporting by Casey Ross and Ike Swetlitz for STAT News (September 2017, "IBM pitched its Watson supercomputer as a revolution in cancer care. It's nowhere close") and confirmed by reporting in IEEE Spectrum and The Verge. The $62 million figure is from MD Anderson's own financial disclosures.

Chapter 3 — The Early Movers Rewrite Reality

Elizabeth Eisenstein's scholarship on the printing press is collected in The Printing Press as an Agent of Change (Cambridge University Press, 1979), condensed into The Printing Revolution in Early Modern Europe (Cambridge University Press, 1983). The social and intellectual consequences of the Gutenberg press are further explored in Adrian Johns's The Nature of the Book (University of Chicago Press, 1998). The Moderna mRNA vaccine design timeline is drawn from the company's own published accounts and from Damian Garde and Jonathan Saltzman's reporting in STAT News (November 2020, "The story of mRNA: How a once-dismissed idea became a leading technology in the Covid vaccine race").

Chapter 4 — Expertise Will Not Belong to Experts

Frederick Winslow Taylor's arguments appear in The Principles of Scientific Management (Harper & Brothers, 1911), available in numerous modern editions. The social consequences of scientific management are examined in Robert Kanigel's The One Best Way: Frederick Winslow Taylor and the Enigma of Efficiency (Viking, 1997). Amazon's automated hiring algorithm and the circumstances of its discontinuation are documented in Jeffrey Dastin's reporting for Reuters (October 2018, "Amazon scraps secret AI recruiting tool that showed bias against women").

Chapter 5 — The Contract That Quietly Expired

The post-war social contract is analysed in Robert Putnam's Bowling Alone: The Collapse and Revival of American Community (Simon & Schuster, 2000). The erosion of long-term employment is documented in Peter Cappelli's The New Deal at Work: Managing the Market-Driven Workforce (Harvard Business School Press, 1999).

Chapter 6 — Education After Memorization

The history of the one-room schoolhouse and the emergence of mass public education is drawn from David Tyack's The One Best System: A History of American Urban Education (Harvard University Press, 1974). Ken Robinson's argument for reforming education is made in Out of Our Minds: Learning to be Creative (Capstone, 2001) and its subsequent editions. Khan Academy's Khanmigo and the design philosophy behind its question-asking approach are described in Khan Academy's own published documentation and in reporting by Kevin Roose in The New York Times (May 2023, "Alarmed by A.I. Chatbots, Universities Start Revamping How They Teach"). Early efficacy assessments should be understood as preliminary.

Chapter 7 — When Work Stops Defining Worth

Henry Ford's $5 workday and its consequences are described in Allan Nevins and Frank Ernest Hill's Ford: The Times, the Man, the Company (Scribner, 1954). Hannah Arendt's analysis of work, labour, and action appears in The Human Condition (University of Chicago Press, 1958), one of the most important political philosophy texts of the twentieth century. The Klarna AI customer service figures — the 700-agent equivalence and two-thirds of chats handled — are drawn from statements made by CEO Sebastian Siemiatkowski in February 2024, reported in Bloomberg and widely covered in subsequent press. The passage focuses on what the company's own metrics revealed and what they did not measure; it does not make claims about subsequent hiring decisions.

Chapter 8 — Democracy Under Cognitive Pressure

The history of Martin Luther's Ninety-Five Theses and the role of the printing press in the Reformation is analysed in Diarmaid MacCulloch's The Reformation: A History (Viking, 2003). The relationship between communication technology and democratic institutions is examined in Eli Pariser's The Filter Bubble (Penguin Press, 2011) and Zeynep Tufekci's Twitter and Tear Gas (Yale University Press, 2017). The Slovak election deepfake audio case is documented in reporting by Reuters and AP Fact Check (September 2023); the Electoral Commission's and independent fact-checkers' findings are publicly available. The timing and spread of the audio, and the electoral outcome, are matters of public record.

Chapter 9 — Who Actually Owns the Future?

Ida Tarbell's investigation of Standard Oil was serialised in McClure's Magazine between 1902 and 1904 and collected as The History of the Standard Oil Company (McClure, Phillips & Co., 1904), available in modern reprint editions. Ron

Chernow's Titan: The Life of John D. Rockefeller, Sr. (Random House, 1998) provides a comprehensive biographical account. Estonia's X-Road system is documented extensively by the Estonian Information System Authority (ria.ee) and has been the subject of academic study; an accessible overview is available from the e-Estonia digital society briefings (e-estonia.com). Liia Hänni's work on the architectural principles behind X-Road is the authoritative source for the design philosophy described here.

Chapter 10 — Most AI Ethics Conversations Are Superficial

The tobacco industry's strategic response to scientific findings is documented in Robert Proctor's Golden Holocaust: Origins of the Cigarette Catastrophe and the Case for Abolition (University of California Press, 2011) and Allan Brandt's The Cigarette Century (Basic Books, 2007). The internal tobacco industry document containing the phrase "Doubt is our product" was produced by the Brown & Williamson Tobacco Corporation and is available in the Legacy Tobacco Documents Library at the University of California, San Francisco. The COMPAS recidivism algorithm and its racial disparity patterns are documented in the ProPublica investigation by Julia Angwin, Jeff Larson, Surya Mattu, and Lauren Kirchner (May 2016, "Machine Bias"); the developer's response and the resulting methodological debate are accessible in subsequent publications in the journal Science (Corbett-Davies et al., 2017). The Air Canada chatbot ruling is documented in the British Columbia Civil Resolution Tribunal decision Moffatt v. Air Canada, 2024 BCCRT 149 (February 2024), publicly available.

Chapter 11 — Dharma, Not Drama

The Bhagavad Gita is available in dozens of English translations; Barbara Stoler Miller's translation (Bantam Books, 1986) is highly regarded for its scholarly accuracy, while Stephen Mitchell's version (Harmony Books, 2000) is more poetic. The historical and philosophical context of the Gita is explored in Wendy Doniger's The Hindus: An Alternative History (Penguin Press, 2009).

Chapter 12 — The World My Daughter Will Inherit

The Imperial War Museum holds extensive collections of letters from both World Wars; their online archive (iwm.org.uk) provides access to selected items. The specific letter referenced in this chapter is drawn from Michael Moynihan's edited collection People at War 1914–1918 (David & Charles, 1973). The letter is reproduced here as it appears in Moynihan's edition. Leonard died in 1943; his correspondence has since entered the public domain. The passage on hope in Chapter 12 is a paraphrase of the argument in Rebecca Solnit's Hope in the Dark: Untold Histories, Wild Possibilities (Haymarket Books, 2004; updated edition 2016). Readers are encouraged to seek out Solnit's original text, which develops this idea with characteristic depth and precision. The epigraph ("We do not inherit the earth from our ancestors...") is widely attributed as a Native American proverb, though its precise origin is disputed; no specific tribe or oral tradition has been definitively identified as the source. The WHO Ethics and Governance of AI in Health guidance document (June 2021) is available in full from the World Health Organization's website (who.int); the six principles described are taken directly from that document.

Chapter 13 — A Day in the Years Ahead

The epigraph is from the Bhagavad Gita, Chapter 2, verse 47 — one of the Gita's central statements on action and detachment from outcome. The Gita is an ancient Sanskrit text and is in the public domain in all translations. Barbara Stoler Miller's translation (Bantam Books, 1986) renders this verse with particular clarity.

Chapter 14 — Alignment Is the Only Scalable Power

The Great Law of the Haudenosaunee and the seventh-generation principle are discussed in Oren Lyons's contribution to Exiled in the Land of the Free: Democracy, Indian Nations, and the U.S. Constitution (Clear Light Publishers, 1992). The influence of the Haudenosaunee Confederacy on American constitutional thinking is examined in Bruce Johansen's Forgotten Founders: Benjamin Franklin, the Iroquois and the Rationale for the American Revolution (Gambit, 1982). New York City Local Law 144 (2021, effective 2023) is publicly available and its implementation is overseen by the NYC Department of Consumer and Worker Protection.

The law's requirements and the independent audit framework are described in the DCWP's official publications.

Further Reading

For readers wishing to go deeper on the core themes of this book, the following works are particularly recommended: Nick Bostrom's Superintelligence (Oxford University Press, 2014); Yuval Noah Harari's Homo Deus (Harper, 2017); Kate Crawford's Atlas of AI (Yale University Press, 2021); Safiya Umoja Noble's Algorithms of Oppression (NYU Press, 2018); Virginia Eubanks's Automating Inequality (St. Martin's Press, 2018); and Cathy O'Neil's Weapons of Math Destruction (Crown, 2016).

On the broader question of technology and human values, Albert Borgmann's Technology and the Character of Contemporary Life (University of Chicago Press, 1984) remains essential.

www.ingramcontent.com/pod-product-compliance
Lightning Source LLC
LaVergne TN
LVHW100136061126
851857LV00010B/117